Aircraft of the
Battle of Britain

John G. Bentley

RAVETTE PUBLISHING

First published in 2010

by Ravette Publishing Limited
PO Box 876
Horsham
West Sussex RH12 9GH

ISBN: 978-1-84161-339-0

Aircraft of the Battle of Britain

Contents

Forward

Since the first model aircraft, that of a Supermarine Spitfire, was produced by Airfix in 1955, a range of models depicting the aircraft which fought in the Battle of Britain have been introduced for aircraft modelling enthusiasts.

Statistically, three generations of men and boys have had the opportunity to build and enjoy the models which represent both the RAF and Luftwaffe aircraft which fought in the skies over Southern England during the summer of 1940.

The first clashes between these Air Forces had taken place over Northern Europe between September 1939 and May 1940, when the RAF had supported the British Expeditionary Force. This Force had been despatched to help Britain's Allies from the onslaught of superior Nazi forces. However, despite the attempts of the combined French and British forces, the might of the German Third Reich was quickly successful in taking control of Poland, Luxemburg, Holland, Norway and France too, leaving the British Expeditionary Force stranded on the beaches of Dunkirk.

A brave and desperate effort involving the combined strength of the Royal Navy, Merchant Navy and many commercial and privately owned yachts, motor launches and small boats successfully brought back over 338,000 men from across the English Channel. 'Operation Dynamo' was a success - but as newly elected Prime Minister Winston Churchill was quick to point out, 'wars are not won by evacuations'.

A Junkers Ju 87 'Stuka' Dive bomber, typical of those used to bomb allied troops as they awaited evacuation from the beaches of Dunkirk. Cat # A05100

The protection provided by the Royal Air Force during that evacuation was crucial in helping to preserve the fighting capability of the British Army. Numerous stories of heroism and miraculous escapes from the Luftwaffe's machine gun strafing and bombing raids came back to British shores with the men.

Determined to quell any expectation that Britain might join the other European nations in succumbing to the might of the German onslaught, Churchill delivered one of the first of several 'immortal' speeches to a packed House of Commons on the 18th of June 1940.

He firstly outlined the states of readiness of the three Armed Services: the Army which had been successfully evacuated from Dunkirk and was now re-grouped and rearmed, the Navy which was materially and tactically ready to fend off any invasion threat, and the Air Force which although numerically was weaker than the Germans, had already achieved a superior record of success in combat. He then went on to say:

What General Weygand called the Battle of France is over. The Battle of Britain is about to begin. Upon this battle depends the survival of Christian civilization. Upon it depends our own British life, and the long continuity of our institutions and our Empire. The whole fury and might of the enemy must very soon be turned on us. Hitler knows that he will have to break us in this Island or lose the war. If we can stand up to

Winston Churchill displays his belief and calls to the nation to unite until 'victory' has been won.

him, all Europe may be free and the life and the world may move forward into broad, sunlit uplands. But if we fail, then the whole world, including the United States, including all that we have known and cared for, will sink into the abyss of a new Dark Age made more sinister, and perhaps more protracted, by the lights of perverted science. Let us therefore brace ourselves to our duties, and so bear ourselves that, if the British Empire and its Commonwealth last for a thousand years, men will still say, "This was their finest hour."

The stage was now set for the start of an epic battle in the skies over Southern England and the English Channel. For a period of intense aerial combat never before seen in human history and never seen since.

Believing that Britain would negotiate for peace and that she was not Germany's natural enemy, Adolf Hitler, acting against the advice of his generals and air commanders did not order the start of that battle for nearly another month. This delay gave the Royal Air Force valuable time to prepare its aircraft and men for the battle that was to come.

However, in early July 1940, Hitler was presented with revised invasion plans by General Jodl, accepted by all of his general staff. Unable to justify delaying any longer, the battle for Britain's air space commenced on July 10th 1940. It was a battle which at any one time could involve up to six hundred RAF aircraft and in the months that followed would see over 2,500 RAF pilots fight for the freedom of the world from the onslaught of Nazi tyranny. Of these, over five hundred were to lose their lives as the two Air Forces battled desperately for air superiority.

The RAF pilots predominantly fought in the new RAF fighters, the Hawker Hurricane and the Supermarine Spitfire, both single-seat fighters each with eight Browning 0.303 calibre machine guns mounted in their wings.

In addition, three other RAF aircraft contributed to the success of the RAF in the Battle of Britain and one aircraft serving with the Fleet Air Arm. The twin and three-seat RAF fighters were the Boulton-Paul Defiant and the Bristol Blenheim. An ageing fighter, the Gloster Gladiator biplane and the Fleet Air Arm's two-seat long-range fighter, the Fairey Fulmar also contributed to the action. Aircraft such as the Wellington and Short Sunderland played support roles.

The Supermarine Spitfire (Cat # A05115) engaging Messerschmitt Bf 109 fighters over England

Heinkel He 111 heavy bomber, predominantly used to bomb Britain from Norway and France (image shown is of a later variant. Cat # A05021)

The Luftwaffe predominantly brought only six types of aircraft into service over the shores of Great Britain including its much feared twin-seat Stuka dive bomber, the Junkers Ju 88 bomber, the Dornier Do 17 and Heinkel He 111 heavy bomber.

Protection of the bombers was initially assigned to the Messerschmitt Bf 110 twin-seat fighter and the faster, more agile and well proven Messerschmitt Bf 109E single-seat fighter. However, as the Battle of Britain progressed, in the same way as the RAF found that its twin-seat Defiants and Bristol Blenheims had selected

and limited use, so also did the Luftwaffe who found the Bf 110 too slow and cumbersome to provide substantial defence against the Hurricane and Spitfire. As a result, most of the battle was fought by RAF pilots in Hurricanes and Spitfires intercepting the Luftwaffe's Messerschmitt Bf 109 fighters as they provided fighter cover to the Heinkel, Junkers and Dornier bombers.

All of the front-line aircraft together with most of the support aircraft which indirectly contributed to the RAF and Luftwaffe's battle for supremacy between July 10th and October 31st 1940, are depicted in well-designed and accurately crafted, ready-to-assemble models in 1/72 scale.

Spitfire Mark 1s and Messerschmitt Bf 109Es in a dogfight over England. (From Cat # A50022)

For 2010, some **new 1/72 scale models** have been introduced including the following aircraft models, each representing aircraft which fought in the Battle of Britain:-

Heinkel He 111	Cat # A05021
Junkers Ju 87B 'Stuka'	Cat # A03030A
Junkers Ju 88 Bomber	Cat # A03007
Spitfire Mk 1A	Cat # A01071A
Messerschmitt Bf 109E	Cat # A02048A
Messerschmitt Bf 110C	Cat # A03080

In addition, other **1/72 scale models** are available to complete the set of twelve Airfix models which represent the twelve main aircraft which fought during the Battle of Britain:-

Gloster Gladiator	Cat # A01002
Boulton Paul Defiant	Cat # A01031
Fairey Fulmar (FAA)	Cat # A02008
Hawker Hurricane Mark 1	Cat # A02096
Bristol Blenheim	Cat # A02027
Dornier Do 17	Cat # A04014

Heinkel He 111s being attacked by Hawker Hurricanes. (From Cat # A50022)

Four of the best known Battle of Britain aircraft, those which represent the most numerous aircraft seen in the skies above Britain in 1940 are also available in **1/48 scale models**:-

Spitfire Mark 1	Cat # A12001
Hurricane Mark 1	Cat # A14102
Messerschmitt Bf 109E	Cat # A05120
Junkers Ju 87 Stuka	Cat # A05100

A superb **1/24 scale model** of the RAF's Mark 1 Hawker Hurricane and Spitfire Mark 1/1a are also available for enthusiasts who enjoy a larger, more detailed model option.

Hawker Hurricane   Cat # A14002
Supermarine Spitfire   Cat # A12001

Supermarine Spitfires fly line astern, commemorating fighter ace Squadron Leader Douglas Bader who flew as a Wing Commander with 12 Group during the Battle of Britain.

These RAF 1/24 scale models are complimented by 1/24 scale models of the Luftwaffe's Junkers Ju 87B 'Stuka' Dive Bomber and Messerschmitt Bf 109E:

Junkers Ju 87B Stuka   Cat # A18002
Messerschmitt Bf 109E   Cat # A12002

New for 2010:

Airfix are pleased to announce a new 2010 70th Anniversary Battle of Britain commemorative set which comprises of four of the most recognisable aircraft from the summer of 1940 in one special edition commemorative gift set. This special anniversary gift set features the…

Heinkel He 111 Bomber
Hawker Hurricane
Supermarine Spitfire and
Messerschmitt Bf 109   Cat # A50022

Still available:

- The Battle of Britain Memorial Flight 1/72 scale models of the Spitfire, Hurricane and Lancaster Bomber   Cat # A50116

- Twin Model Gift Set: 'Dogfight Double' Junkers Ju 88 and Hawker Hurricane 1/72 scale   Cat # A50038

Above: The Boulton Paul Defiant

Below: The Gloster Gladiator

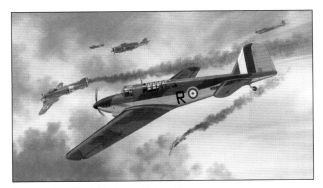

Above: The Fleet Air Arm's Fairey Fulmar

Below: The Hawker Hurricane

Above: The Dornier Do 17 Bomber

Below: The Messerschmitt Bf 109E Single-Seat Fighter

Further collectable scale models from the Battle of Britain era include:-

RAF Airfield Set
(1/72 scale)   Cat # A06901

Battle of Britain Airfield Set
(New - 1/72 scale featuring the Supermarine Spitfire Mark 1A, two refuelling vehicles, airfield personnel and paints, brushes and adhesive)
                                          Cat # A50015

Luftwaffe Airfield Set
(1/72 scale)   Cat # A06902
Luftwaffe Personnel
(New - 1/72 scale)   Cat # A01755

The Opposing Forces:
Operational Strength at July 10th 1940

RAF Aircraft Strength (all aircraft)
1,963 serviceable aircraft
including 708 fighters

Luftwaffe Strength (all aircraft)
4,074 serviceable aircraft
including 1,200 fighters and 1,750 bombers

The Birth of a Military Aircraft

Until recent years, every military aircraft started its life with a design being submitted to the respective Air Ministry. Each design was required to meet an aircraft specification laid down in advance by the Ministry. That specification called for specific minimum requirements to be met. The specification could be broad in many aspects (for example 'to reach a minimum speed of 250 mph') but might also be very detailed in others.

If the Air Ministry concerned approved the soundness and relevance of the conceptual design, the usual way forward for the life of that aircraft was to move to the 'build' stage with the grant of development funding sufficient to produce at least one (but more likely two or three) prototypes.

At the specification stage the manufacturer would recommend the make and model of engine it considered suitable to propel the aircraft. These would normally be selected from the most recent engines created by established and respected engine manufacturers of which Rolls Royce, Bristol, Pratt & Whitney, Daimler-Benz, Fiat and BMW were the most significant in the late 1930s.

Numerous manufacturers might tender designs for the same Air Ministry specification. In that case the Ministry would conduct comparison tests to see which design it would like to see taken through to production.

There were very few exceptions to this procedure before the start of the Second World War. Those exceptions usually were where the foresight of the Air Ministry recognised qualities contained in a civil aircraft as being adaptable for military use. In such cases the cost of development could be reduced. If the aircraft manufacturer 'won' a contract to manufacture the aircraft, initial orders would be placed enabling that company to develop and to equip its factory for mass production.

Aircraft Manufacturers in 1938

After the First World War the League of Nations had been overseeing Germany's economic and industrial recovery with a view to ensuring that the military might of that nation could not be restored.

Under the supervision of the German government, the most prominent pre-war aircraft manufacturers in Germany had therefore developed aircraft for civil use. However most German designs were in practice, capable of easy military adaptation. German pilots had been trained to fly in gliding and sport clubs as well as by civil aviation companies.

By 1936-37, the German civil air force had an abundance of aircraft suitable for 'delivering the post' with crews of 3-6 men per aircraft. Sports and potential record-breaking performance aircraft were being designed with speed and maneuverability in mind. This was all as magicians say, 'smoke and mirrors'. The German government was building the infrastructure for the re-birth of a military air force where the 'post' became bombs and 'sport' became the ability for aircraft to duel in the air. Junkers, Heinkel and Dornier were leading manufacturers of civil aircraft in Germany at this time and Messerschmitt of sports and performance aircraft.

In England such deception was not needed. Hawker, Fairey, Bristol and Avro were already leading manufacturers of military aircraft and both Supermarine and Shorts had established themselves as pioneers in float-plane development. Supermarine focussed on high-speed aircraft capable of winning the coveted Schneider Trophy for attaining air-speed records.

The Testing under Combat Conditions

Throughout the late 1930s the major aircraft manufacturers of Europe were creating newer and more advanced designs to meet the increasingly high demands of their respective governments. This was not just the case in Britain and Germany, but in all the major nations of the world. What was unknown by

each nation was how those aircraft would compare with those built by opposing countries, should those nations find themselves at war with each other.

The Spanish Civil War gave the German and Italian nations a chance to test their aircraft in a hostile environment whereas Britain's and France's pre-war development and technology remained unproven until the hostilities commenced in September 1939. When this occurred, it was quickly recognised that only one French Fighter – the Dewoitine D.520 was any match for the Messerschmitt Bf 109. The RAF did not commit its latest aircraft, the Spitfire to the French cause in 1939. Of the aircraft committed, only the Hurricane proved a worthy opponent to the Bf 109 which now looked as though it might be the best fighter aircraft in the world.

Under combat conditions, a huge number of variables were soon to be tested; which bombers had the best combination of defensive and aggressive armament? Which fighters had the best overall performance in a dogfight situation? Which fighters were best suited to bomber escort duties? Which aircraft were most suited to night time operations? And which aircraft could be manufactured and delivered in time to meet the increasing demands of their respective governments?

In just a few weeks during the summer of 1940, all of these questions were to be answered.

Junkers Ju 87 (Stuka)

First conceived in 1933, the Junker Ju 87 Stuka was a remarkably successful dive-bomber that remained in production until 1944. More than 5,700 'Stuka' bombers were completed in twelve differing versions during that eleven years and it became one of the most widely used combat aircraft of the Luftwaffe.

Although ugly and awkward looking, this aircraft played a primary role in the aggressive Luftwaffe tactics of the early war as a dive-bomber. It quickly became known to both Allied and Axis forces to represent the Luftwaffe's agility, diversity and strength.

The Stuka (which is short for Sturzkampfflugzeug) is the German word for dive-bomber. It was used in Germany to describe all forms of dive-bomber. However the Ju 87 was promoted within Germany to symbolise the Blitzkrieg (lightning war) which enabled Germany to dominate the first months of the Second World War and it soon became known across Europe simply as 'the Stuka'.

In addition to its fighting potential, the sound it generated while diving to attack was an eerie whistling sound. This struck fear into the hearts of those below, knowing it carried certain death to those in the sights of the pilot who also doubled up as the bomb aimer.

Even when the myth surrounding this aircraft faded, it remained irreplaceable in its role; so much so that the German aircraft industry proved incapable of producing a substitute despite the significant progress in aircraft design made during the course of the war.

The Junkers Ju 87 project was launched in response to a demand for the construction of an aircraft to be used as a tactical twin-seat dive-bomber. Of the four manufacturers who set about designing such a plane, the Junkers design proved most effective and in March 1936, after an extensive series of comparative tests, the Ju 87 prototype was chosen for production. The aircraft, designed by Hermann Pohlmann, made its maiden flight in early 1935, but during the months that followed it was significantly modified and updated.

The original prototype had been easily recognisable by double tailplanes and the use of a British Rolls-Royce Kestrel engine, generating over 500bhp at take off while driving a two-blade wooden propeller.

Early test flights of this version brought to light a significant overheating problem with the Rolls-Royce engines and some structural weakness. A second prototype was developed using a 610bhp Junkers Jumo engine which drove a three-blade variable pitch metal propeller. It also adopted a single tailplane. These major modifications alongside further refinements of detail were incorporated into the third prototype, which provided the basis for the first production version variant of the 'Stuka'.

The Junkers Ju 87 had an all-metal airframe and skin, with wings which had a characteristic "inverted gull" shape. These, along with a fixed landing gear housed in large, sturdy (but not aerodynamic) fairings, gave the Stuka a distinctive appearance from all angles.

The main bomb load was attached to a support under the belly of the fuselage. Early defensive armament consisted of a fixed 7.9 mm forward firing machine gun and a similar weapon in the rear of a fully glazed cockpit.

Sep 1939 - A flight of Stukas demonstrating air superiority over Poland - *Bundesarchiv*

23 Apr 1940 - Norway, Trondheim - Colonel General Erhard Milch soldiers lined up in front of the Air Force - in the background Junkers Ju 87 - *Bundesarchiv*

The first production variant, the Ju 87 A-1, became active in early 1937. After initial use as a trainer, the aircraft saw combat and the opportunity for further refinements to be made during the Spanish Civil War. As a result in 1938, the B-1 was introduced, with a more powerful version of the Jumo engine and with further modifications to the fuselage. This was the first version to be built in any great number and was the variant used in the Battle of Britain to attack radar stations and airfields.

C and D series of the Stuka followed in 1941 with further structural and dynamic improvements (and more powerful engines and greater armament).

The final G version was used from 1942 until the end of the war in 1945, and this variant specialised in anti-tank bombing.

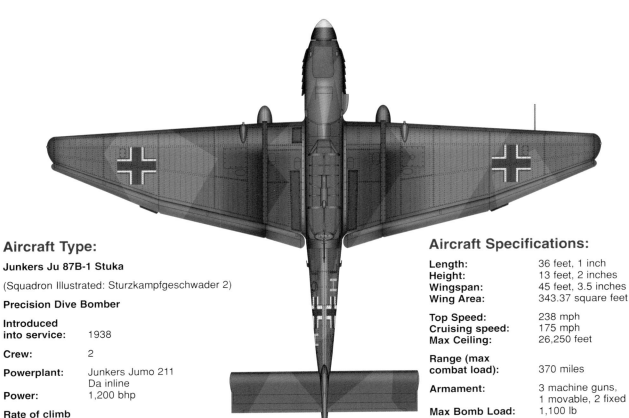

Aircraft Type:

Junkers Ju 87B-1 Stuka

(Squadron Illustrated: Sturzkampfgeschwader 2)

Precision Dive Bomber

**Introduced
into service:**   1938

Crew: 2

Powerplant: Junkers Jumo 211
                    Da inline

Power: 1,200 bhp

**Rate of climb
at take-off:**   1,640 ft/min

Aircraft Specifications:

Length: 36 feet, 1 inch
Height: 13 feet, 2 inches
Wingspan: 45 feet, 3.5 inches
Wing Area: 343.37 square feet

Top Speed: 238 mph
Cruising speed: 175 mph
Max Ceiling: 26,250 feet

**Range (max
combat load):**   370 miles

Armament: 3 machine guns,
                  1 movable, 2 fixed

Max Bomb Load: 1,100 lb

17

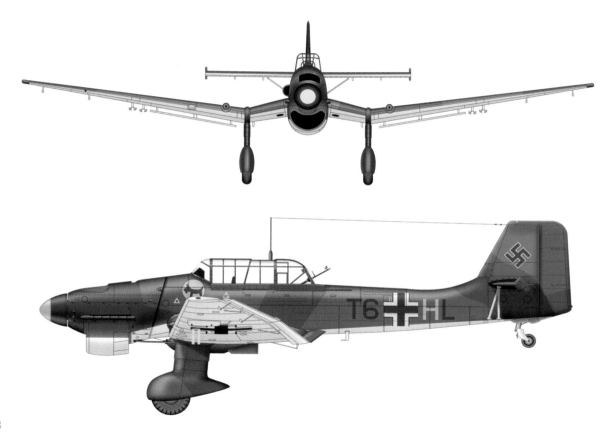

Hawker Hurricane

Although often underrated due to the fame of its more streamline 'compatriot', the Spitfire, the unsung hero of the Battle of Britain was undoubtedly the Hawker Hurricane.

At the outbreak of war, the RAF had 32 Hurricane squadrons compared to 19 Spitfire squadrons. It therefore became not only the most used British fighter during the Battle of Britain, but also the most successful, accounting for nearly three out of every four enemy aircraft shot down over British shores.

Of the 620 Hurricane and Spitfire fighters (with another 84 assorted fighters including the Defiant, Blenheim and Gloster Gladiator) Hurricane squadrons had to face the German air threat of 3,500 bombers and fighters.

The Hurricane was designed by Sydney Camm, who first began work on the aircraft in the late spring of 1934. The prototype first flew in November 1935 at Brooklands, and the production Hurricane Mark 1 entered RAF service in December 1937.

The Hurricane was a remarkable combination of established, well-proven biplane design technology translated into an aircraft that had the performance of a monoplane. Powered by the Rolls-Royce Merlin engine, it became the first RAF monoplane fighter with an enclosed cockpit and retractable undercarriage. It was also the first RAF fighter capable of exceeding 300 mph in level flight.

The Hurricane proved to have an astounding ability for adaptation and the varied roles it undertook throughout the war earned it the distinction of being the most versatile single-seat fighter of the Second World War.

The Hurricane was a clean aircraft, with tubular metal construction and fabric covering, similar to the earlier Hawker Fury biplanes. Many of its contours (including the tail surfaces) were characteristic of previous Camm designs with the continuation of fabric covering a rigid airframe. This was viewed with misgivings by some, and was soon replaced by a metal skin on the wings.

The first Hurricanes were powered by a Rolls Royce Merlin "C" engine, a name that had earlier been given to the PV-12. This drove a Watts two-blade fixed-pitch wooden propeller.

The first squadron to be equipped with a single-seat monoplane fighter was No. 111 Squadron based at Northholt. The delivery of the Hurricane was seen to be progressive and the Hurricane quickly came to symbolise the modern RAF in publicity posters.

Above: The Hawker Hurricane - this World War 2 fully restored Mark 1 is the property of the Historic Aircraft Collection which flies regularly at airshows across the United Kingdom.

During May 1940, the last Hurricanes with fabric-covered wings and wooden fixed-pitched airscrews were scheduled to be withdrawn from all front-line operational squadrons but the heavy losses suffered in Europe through May and June dictated this policy be reversed. Instead, the re-issue of many of the older machines took place.

During the battle of France, during which the Hurricane proved to be the only allied plane capable of holding its own against the mighty Messerschmitt Bf 109E, the RAF's Hurricanes took considerable losses. Between May 10th and June 20th 1940, 386 Hurricanes were lost. After this, Fighter Command had little more than a month to prepare for the Battle of Britain.

Technically, the Hurricane was inferior to the Bf 109E in most performance aspects including speed, rate of climb and rate of dive. However, its low-altitude maneuverability and turning circle at all altitudes meant that provided the Bf 109E didn't have a significant altitude advantage, it was a fair match. Unlike the Messerschmitt, the Hurricane's sturdy structure enabled it to withstand significant firepower - absorbing levels of damage that would have proved the end of many other aircraft.

Unlike in France, the Battle of Britain saw Spitfire squadrons becoming involved in active combat. The Spitfire was considered a more able opponent for the Bf 109 therefore Hurricanes were allocated the primary task of attacking Luftwaffe bomber formations while allowing the faster-climbing Spitfire to deal with the Bf 109E escorts.

In the reality of the intensity of battle though, it was rarely possibly to co-ordinate the separate formations and once engaging the enemy, both Spitfires and Hurricanes alike were consumed in a battle for survival and dominance of the skies.

During the August and September of the Battle of Britain some 696 Hurricanes were lost to enemy action and 503 new machines were delivered. Yet the Order of Battle remained static and Hurricane-equipped squadrons increased to 31, including a Canadian, one Czechoslovakian and two Polish units.

From September 1940 the Hurricane IIA Series was powered by a two-stage supercharged Merlin engine capable of producing 1,206 bhp at 11,750 ft and 1,160 bhp at 20,750 ft. This additional power enabled the Hurricane to remain a significant fighter in the hands of the RAF throughout the war with flying speeds of up to 342 mph.

By the end of October when the Battle of Britain came to an end, the Hurricane had proved to be a fine fighting machine by any standard, providing an excellent and stable gun platform for the eight Browning .303 machine guns with which it was fitted.

Of the 14,533 production Hurricanes built, some went for service with other Air Forces. Nearly 3,000 were dispatched to the Soviet Union to aid its fight against the Germans on the Eastern Front.

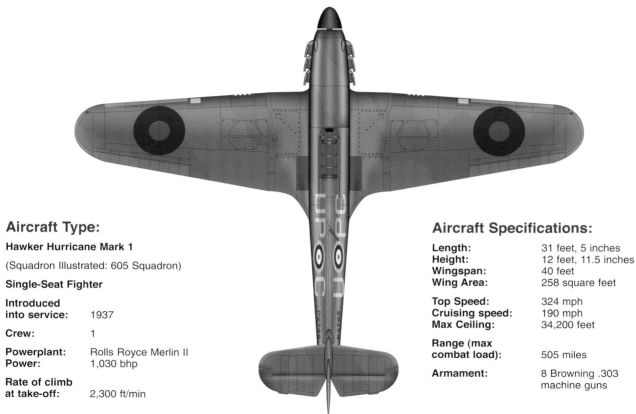

Aircraft Type:

Hawker Hurricane Mark 1

(Squadron Illustrated: 605 Squadron)

Single-Seat Fighter

**Introduced
into service:**   1937

Crew: 1

Powerplant: Rolls Royce Merlin II
Power: 1,030 bhp

**Rate of climb
at take-off:**   2,300 ft/min

Aircraft Specifications:

Length: 31 feet, 5 inches
Height: 12 feet, 11.5 inches
Wingspan: 40 feet
Wing Area: 258 square feet

Top Speed: 324 mph
Cruising speed: 190 mph
Max Ceiling: 34,200 feet

**Range (max
combat load):**   505 miles

Armament: 8 Browning .303
machine guns

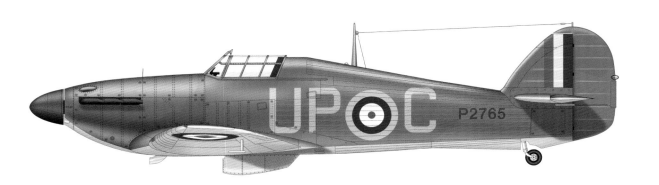

UP●C   P2765

23

Messerschmitt Bf 110

The Messerschmitt Bf 110, was a twin-engine fighter nicknamed 'Zerstörer' (the 'Destroyer'). It was designed to be a multi-purpose long-range fighter which, with adaptation could be capable of delivering a bomb load. This was the requirement laid down by Goering. With an all-metal skin it provided reasonable protection for its crew and could be armed with cannons or machine guns.

Other companies who contended to provide this specification of aircraft to the Luftwaffe included Focke-Wulf and Henschel, whose Fw 57 and Hs 124 were similar in design. Partly because the Bf 110 prototype omitted the ability to carry a bomb-load, it was far superior to its rivals in speed, range and firepower. In early 1937 when faced with the three rival aircraft to choose from, the Luftwaffe made no delay in placing its orders with Messerschmitt.

Despite delivery and performance issues with the DB600 engine (which had initially been selected to power the Bf 110), production commenced in the summer of 1937. Three distinct versions were produced: a fighter, a trainer and a reconnaissance version. The advent of the DB601 engine in 1938 resolved the power plant problems taking the top speed as high as 336 mph and giving it a range of 680 miles.

Although it proved to be a very successful aircraft in the Luftwaffe's early campaigns in Northern Europe and France, this was primarily due to the standard of aircraft deployed by its opponents. The Bf 110 was not an agile aircraft and therefore did not possess one of the integral requirements of a successful fighter. This weakness was fully displayed during the Battle of Britain when it was deployed alongside Dornier, Junkers and Heinkel bombers as a fighter escort. It was no match for the defending Hurricane and Spitfires and Bf 110 squadrons took heavy losses.

In early 1940, Walter Horten, a technical officer, had been invited to participate in a "mock combat" with a Bf 109E. The Bf 109 showed superiority over the Bf 110 consistently and after the test combat, Horten said,

"Gentlemen, be very careful if you should ever come up against the English. Their fighters are all single-engined. And once they get to know the Bf 110's weaknesses, you could be in for a very nasty surprise."

The Bf 110 often violated Swiss airspace during early 1940, so became one of the few aircraft to become a casualty of the Air Force of a neutral country when five Bf 110s were shot down. However, its most significant claim to fame was made in May 1941 when Rudolf Hess, the deputy leader of the Nazi party flew in a

Bf 110 from Munich to Scotland in an attempt to broker peace. He was captured and remained a prisoner of war for the rest of his life.

However, it was unique at the time as a long-range bomber escort, and did not have the problems of restricted range that hampered the Bf 109E. Although outclassed, it was still formidable as an escort for bombers using its ability to dive on enemy fighters from height delivering a long-range burst from its powerful forward-facing armament.

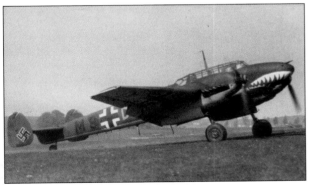

May 1940 - Messerschmitt Bf 110 of the Destroyer Squadron 76 (ZG 76, ID) with shark-foot-painting; KBK Lw 4 - *Bundesarchiv*

Oct 1940 - France - refuelling a Messerschmitt Bf 110 of Destroyer Squadron 26 ZG "Horst Wessel"; KBK 5 Lw - *Bundesarchiv*

Hermann Goering's nephew, Hans-Joachim Goering, was a pilot with III Zerstörergeschwader 76, flying the Messerschmitt Bf 110. Hans-Joachim was killed on 11th July 1940, when his Bf 110 was shot down by Hurricanes of No. 78 Squadron and his aircraft crashed into Portland Harbour, Dorset.

The worst day of the Battle of Britain for the Bf 110 was on 15th August 1940, when nearly 30 Bf 110s were shot down, the equivalent of an entire Gruppe. However, 30th August saw 13 RAF fighters shot down in the Bf 110's most successful day of that summer.

After the Battle of Britain, the Luftwaffe were able to deploy its Bf 110s in other theatres of war which had opened up tactically, utilising its strengths as a ground-support fighter-bomber (Jagdbomber-Jabo), and as a night fighter, a role in which it excelled. Most German night fighter aces flew the Bf 110 during their combat careers, including Major Heinz-Wolfgang Schnaufer who flew it exclusively and claimed a remarkable 121 victories in 164 combat missions.

The Bf 110's main strength was its ability to accept extreme weaponry. Early versions had four 7.92 mm MG 17 machine guns in the upper nose and two 20 mm cannons in the lower part of the nose. Later versions replaced the MG FF/M with more powerful 20 mm cannons and many G-series aircraft which served in the bomber-destroyer role had two 30 mm cannons instead of the MG 17 machine guns. The defensive armament consisted of a single, flexibly-mounted 7.92 mm MG 15 machine gun. Late F-series and prototype G-series aircraft were upgraded to a 7.92 mm MG 81 machine gun which gave a higher rate of fire.

The Bf 110 G-2/R1 was also capable of carrying the Bordkanone series 37 mm cannon. A single hit from this weapon was often found to be enough to destroy any Allied bomber.

The fighter-bomber versions could carry up to 2,000 kg (4,410 lb) of bombs depending on the type.

The Messerschmitt Me 210 entered service in mid 1941, giving subsequent Bf 110 variants the opportunity to meet more specific criteria. The 210 was not a successful aircraft though and was soon withdrawn from service in favour of continuing with Bf 110 development.

21 June 1940 - Western France - Destroyer Squadron 26, middle: Major Johann Schalk, right: Lieutenant Theodore Rossiwal in front of a Messerschmitt Bf 110 - *Bundesarchiv*

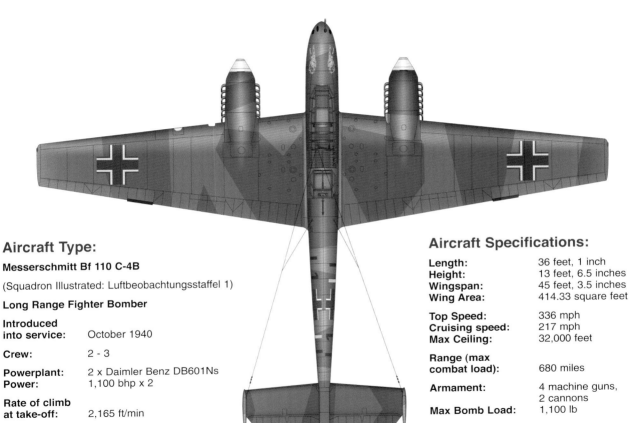

Aircraft Type:

Messerschmitt Bf 110 C-4B

(Squadron Illustrated: Luftbeobachtungsstaffel 1)

Long Range Fighter Bomber

**Introduced
into service:** October 1940

Crew: 2 - 3

Powerplant: 2 x Daimler Benz DB601Ns
Power: 1,100 bhp x 2

**Rate of climb
at take-off:** 2,165 ft/min

Aircraft Specifications:

Length: 36 feet, 1 inch
Height: 13 feet, 6.5 inches
Wingspan: 45 feet, 3.5 inches
Wing Area: 414.33 square feet

Top Speed: 336 mph
Cruising speed: 217 mph
Max Ceiling: 32,000 feet

**Range (max
combat load):** 680 miles

Armament: 4 machine guns,
2 cannons
Max Bomb Load: 1,100 lb

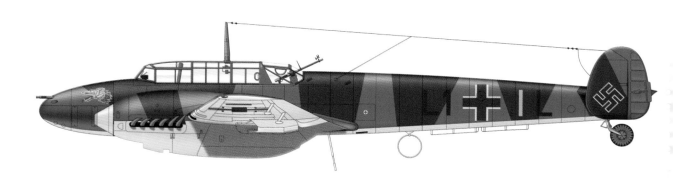

28

Bristol Blenheim Mark I

On September 3, 1939, the RAF carried out its first operative mission of World War 2, which was a reconnaissance flight over Germany. The aircraft used for this historic event was a small and fast medium range bomber – the Bristol Blenheim.

Although the Blenheim was not an outstanding combat aircraft in 1940, it proved to be indispensable in its role until succeeded by the Beaufighter three years later.

More than 5,500 Blenheims were built in two major production versions which fought on almost all fronts. It was also used by the Canadian and South African Air Forces.

The origins of the twin-engine Bristol are still intertwined in British aviation history. The Blenheim came into being in 1934 as an initiative of a successful newspaper publisher, Lord Rothermere, who owned the Daily Mail. Rothermere asked manufacturers to design a fast, modern twin-engine private transport plane, capable of carrying six passengers and two crew members. Rothermere was very explicit in his request: the aircraft was to be "the fastest commercial plane in Europe, if not the world".

This proposal attracted the attention of the Bristol Company, which coincidentally had been working on early designs for an aircraft of this type. The designer, Frank Barnwell, had no hesitation in installing two powerful British Mercury radial engines (each generating 608 bhp) in the airframe. In this configuration, the prototype (designated Type 142) made its first flight in April 1935. It was particularly impressive as far as speed was concerned: during flight tests it reached almost 307 mph which made it superior to that of any other British fighter at the time.

Two months later, impressed by this remarkable design, Rothermere presented it to the nation. The Air Ministry quickly evaluated the aircraft and transformed the prototype into a light bomber. In September 1935 it placed an order for 150 production series aircraft.

However, adapting the aircraft for military use did not prove to be a simple task. It had to be substantially modified, especially the wing structure where the wings had to be raised to provide bomb housing and the fuselage had to be adapted to provide suitable positions for the armament.

The Blenheim was an elegant all-metal aircraft with retractable landing gear. The first prototype flew in June 1936, and subsequent delivery of the aircraft to forward units, commenced in January 1937.

Production continued at a great pace and before passing to the subsequent major production variant – the Mark IV (built at the end of 1938), some 1,552 Blenheim Mark Is had come off the assembly lines.

In the Mark IV, the designers had taken the operative experiences of the aircraft into account so that as well as being provided with additional armament, the number of machine guns could be increased to five and the bomb load to 1,325 lb. More powerful engines (920 bhp Bristol Mercury XVs) were also fitted in the Blenheim Mark IVs.

Structural modifications to the fuselage included a different nose structure and wings that contained larger fuel tanks. The first units began to receive the new variant in March 1939, and 168 Blenheim Mark IVs were in operational squadrons when the war broke out.

Production continued until a total of 3,983 had been completed including the Type 149 version, which although rejected by the RAF, was used by the Canadian Air Force who built it under licence with the name of 'Bolingbroke'. The Bolingbroke was similar to the Blenheim Mark I but powered by different engines. Finally, 945 Mark Vs were produced with further modifications to the armament and fuselage. However, the latter aircraft never proved to be particularly effective.

When it first flew, the Blenheim was faster than any fighter in service with the RAF at the time. This was because it had a relatively small fuselage. However, the pilot's quarters on the left side of the nose were so cramped that the control yoke obscured all flight instruments while engine instruments eliminated the forward view on landings and by 1940 it was a slow aircraft compared to the single-seat fighters operating in the same airspace.

The cramped cockpit of the Bristol Blenheim

In its role as a fast, light bomber, Blenheim units raided German occupied airfields throughout July to December 1940, both during daylight hours and at night. Due to its speed, there were some missions which produced an almost 100% casualty rate amongst the Blenheims. It is a testament to the courage of the aircrews that they continued to operate throughout these months without significant credit from Fighter Command.

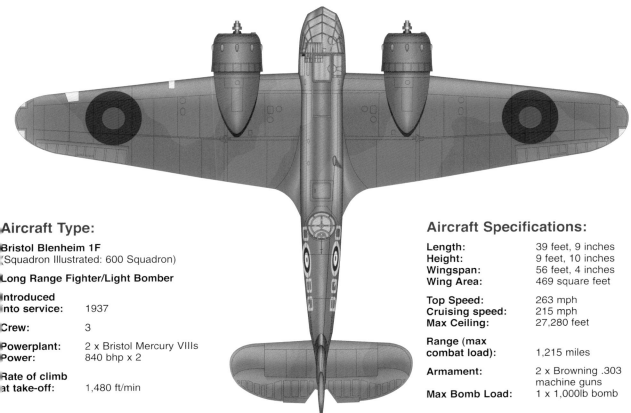

Aircraft Type:

Bristol Blenheim 1F
(Squadron Illustrated: 600 Squadron)

Long Range Fighter/Light Bomber

**Introduced
into service:** 1937

Crew: 3

Powerplant: 2 x Bristol Mercury VIIIs
Power: 840 bhp x 2

**Rate of climb
at take-off:** 1,480 ft/min

Aircraft Specifications:

Length:	39 feet, 9 inches
Height:	9 feet, 10 inches
Wingspan:	56 feet, 4 inches
Wing Area:	469 square feet
Top Speed:	263 mph
Cruising speed:	215 mph
Max Ceiling:	27,280 feet
Range (max combat load):	1,215 miles
Armament:	2 x Browning .303 machine guns
Max Bomb Load:	1 x 1,000lb bomb

31

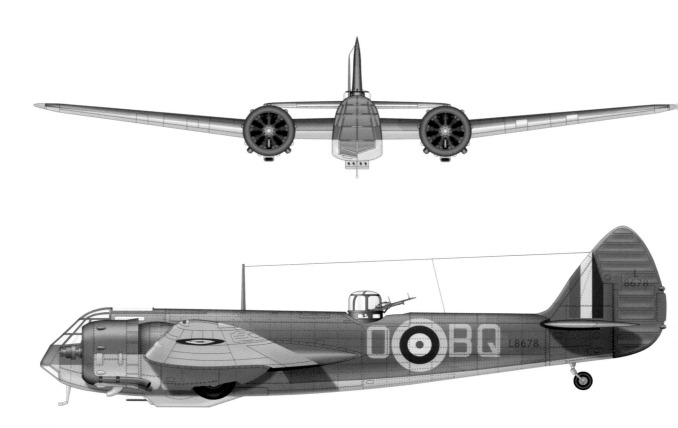

Boulton Paul Defiant

Air Ministry specification F.9/35 required the design of a two-seat fighter in which the pilot would occupy the front seat while a specialist gunner would occupy a rear turret. Few pitches were made for such an aircraft but Boulton Paul considered their existing work as being complimentary to such a design and forwarded plans for the Boulton Paul Defiant. These designs were accepted by the Air Ministry in June 1934.

Initial delays in production meant that the first Defiants did not enter RAF service until December 1939, by which time many pilots were used to the performance of the single-seat Spitfire and the Hurricane, each with four wing-fixed .303 Browing machine guns. Nevertheless, the potential of a rear gunner in a rotating turret on a similar airframe to the Hurricane suggested that the Defiant had a good future when placed in the right role.

The maximum speed was a little over 300 mph at a 17,000 ft ceiling, again quite respectable - but the main disadvantage was that the turret was ideally positioned for rear and side fire only. The turret also restricted the aircraft's maneuverability and gave virtually no forward firing power at all.

One of the main failings in the design of the Defiant was the consideration given to the rear gunner, who needed to be very small in height and build to be able to access his position in the gun turret. In addition the gunner had to wear specially designed flying clothes capable of having the Mae West (life jacket) down one trouser leg and the parachute down the other.

Access to the turret while the aircraft was on the ground was difficult, but possible with the guns facing in a direction other than in the normal firing position. Once inside, the gunner had very little possibility of movement. In the event of an emergency, the only way to escape was through a small emergency hatch. Emergencies were commonplace though and as a result, gunners on the Defiant were lost at a rate of two to one compared to pilots. In fact the design of the special flying suit meant that if the gunner was able to escape the aircraft while in the water, the pull of the Mae West and parachute inverted him and he was likely to drown unless able to free himself from both items in a matter of seconds.

The first squadron to fly the Defiant was newly formed 264 Squadron operating out of RAF Sutton Bridge (and then from Martlesham Heath). The squadron was sent to France to help the RAF's efforts there.

Making its first appearance at Dunkirk during the evacuation of the British Expeditionary Force, the squadron of Defiants was mistakenly thought to have been

Hurricanes. Messerschmitt Bf 109s attacked from above and the rear, which proved to be a grave mistake. The rear facing turret gunners in the Defiants showed how competent the design was to counter the classic attack of this kind. However, the 'turret fighter' (as it became known) was now revealed to the Bf 109 pilots, and the Luftwaffe soon found that the aircraft's weaknesses were in fact being attacked from the front and from below.

Boulton Paul Defiant Mark I aircraft from No. 264 Squadron at dispersal at Kirton-in-Lindsey. They were later withdrawn and moved to night patrol missions - *Francois Prins*

141 Squadron was also equipped with Defiants. During this squadron's first sortie over Folkestone it was attacked by a formation of Bf 109s just off the coastline. The Bf 109s shot down two Defiants with their first pass and returned to down four more on a second pass. The Luftwaffe had learned their lesson. In August 1940, 264 Squadron suffered a similar fate.

The Defiant was to prove that as a fighter with poor maneuverability and with all its armament concentrated in a rear-facing turret instead of in the wings, was tactically flawed. It was not suited to the intensity of operations and style of attack that was taking place during the summer of 1940.

After 264 Squadron's experience, the aircraft was withdrawn from daylight combat operations. However, the RAF did find a role which it was well suited for. Fitted with radar and operating at night, it became extremely successful as a night fighter, shooting down more raiders per interception than any other night fighter during 1940-1941.

The Defiant continued on as a night fighter and as a special operations aircraft used for radar jamming and special operations until 1944 when the twin-engine Mosquito finally replaced it.

The Defiant was not successful in its role during the Battle of Britain, but it is clear that had it been operational five years earlier, it would have been seen to be a fine aircraft.

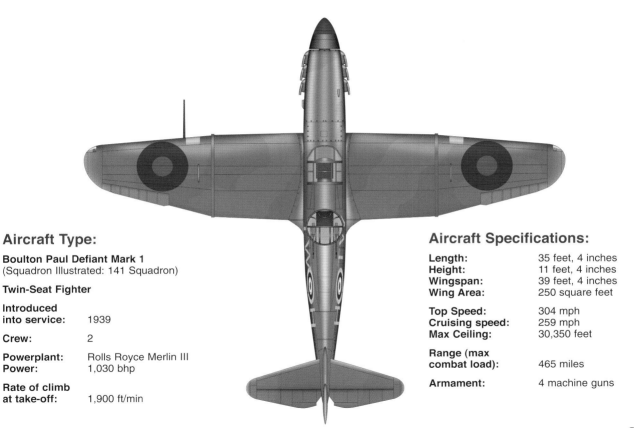

Aircraft Type:

Boulton Paul Defiant Mark 1
(Squadron Illustrated: 141 Squadron)

Twin-Seat Fighter

**Introduced
into service:** 1939

Crew: 2

Powerplant: Rolls Royce Merlin III
Power: 1,030 bhp

**Rate of climb
at take-off:** 1,900 ft/min

Aircraft Specifications:

Length: 35 feet, 4 inches
Height: 11 feet, 4 inches
Wingspan: 39 feet, 4 inches
Wing Area: 250 square feet

Top Speed: 304 mph
Cruising speed: 259 mph
Max Ceiling: 30,350 feet

**Range (max
combat load):** 465 miles

Armament: 4 machine guns

35

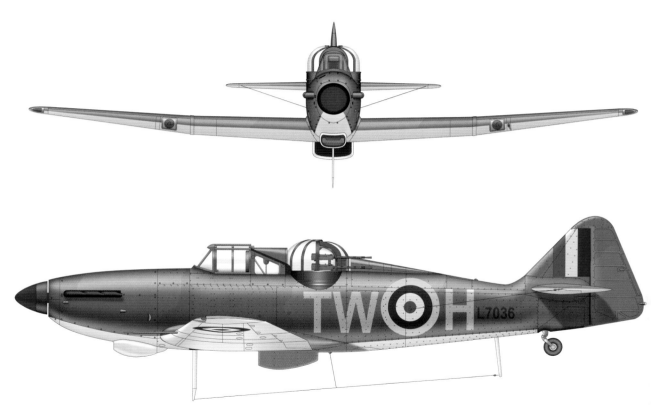

Messerschmitt Bf 109

Designed by 'Willy' Messerschmitt, the Bf 109 was an inspired and tidy fighter which, like the Supermarine Spitfire, had ruthless efficiency.

It was a modern aircraft which took full advantage of the most advanced aerodynamic and structural stressed-skin construction with high wing loading. This was compensated for with slotted 'trailing' flaps.

The Bf 109 gave its pilots superb handling and response at both low and medium speeds. Its climbing and diving performance was second to none but maneuverability was inferior to the Spitfire and Hurricane. Its failing was that the controls became heavier at speed due to the absence of a rudder trimmer. This meant the pilots had to constantly adjust the rudder to fly straight at high speeds.

The Bf 109 was first flown in 1935 and like many Luftwaffe aircraft, was successfully tested and proved in the Spanish Civil War.

The Bf 109E was the first true mass production model and was able to outfight or perform most of its opposition. The Daimler-Benz 601 engine used a fuel injection system instead of a carburettor, which enabled it to function under negative 'G' without spluttering or stalling, a distinct advantage over opponents during the summer of 1940.

Some 'E' models were equipped with four MG 17 machine guns and the remainder with two MG 17s in the fuselage and two MG FF cannons in the wing roots. There was also a light bomber version, the Bf 109E-1/B which was fitted with racks for 4 x 110 lb or one 550 lb bomb.

At the start of the Battle of Britain, the Bf 109E was given the task of countering British fighters on a one to one basis while the two-seat Messerschmitt Bf 110 acted as an escort for the bomber formations. It was therefore able to take full advantage of the climbing and diving capabilities.

Although several variants were made, some were not significant improvements on the original concept of a high performance fighter which was well interpreted in the E series.

Due to the vulnerability of the Bf 110 when confronted with Hurricanes and Spitfires, Bf 109s were soon assigned as escorts to protect the bomber formations. The strict limitations placed on the tactics of the Bf 109s meant they were unable to use their speed advantage, and they could be out-turned by both the Hurricane and Spitfire.

With increasing casualties being suffered by the bomber formations, Goering insisted the Bf 109s stayed closer to the bombers, rendering them even more vulnerable.

Fighting in the skies of Southern England with its limited tactical radius put it at a constant disadvantage, but its performance and armament were formidable. Of the 610 Bf 109Es lost during the Battle of Britain, ten percent had run out of fuel during or after combat. The limited range also restricted its ability to act as a bomber escort.

The Bf 109F was therefore devised as a lighter aircraft, achieving the weight reduction and an increase in range through reducing the armament. This compromised the fighter abilities but did make it more suited to bomber escort duties.

Sep 1939 - Messerschmitt Bf 109s assembled on a captured Polish airfield - *Bundesarchiv*

1939 - Luftwaffe soldiers of the Jagdgeschwader 53 (JG 53) fighter wing (also known as "Ace of Spades") resting at an airfield in front of a Messerschmitt Bf 109 with an open bonnet. Behind in the background is a Junkers Ju 52 transport - *Bundesarchiv*

The Bf 109s were withdrawn from assault at the end of October, their pilots (as with their British counterparts) suffering from physical and nervous strain.

By the end of the war, the Bf 109 had become an aged design yet remained the backbone of the German Air Force's day fighter force and was flown by many of her allies.

Like the Spitfire, the Bf 109 saw action throughout the war. More than 33,000 were built in total, a figure only superseded by the Russian 'Sturmovik'.

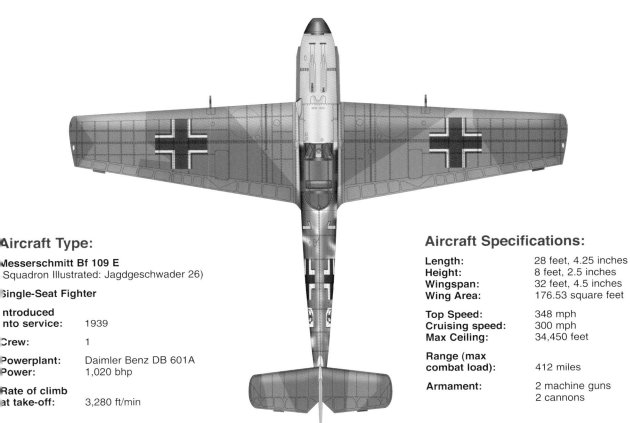

Aircraft Type:

Messerschmitt Bf 109 E
(Squadron Illustrated: Jagdgeschwader 26)

Single-Seat Fighter

**Introduced
into service:**   1939

Crew: 1

Powerplant: Daimler Benz DB 601A
Power: 1,020 bhp

**Rate of climb
at take-off:**   3,280 ft/min

Aircraft Specifications:

Length:	28 feet, 4.25 inches
Height:	8 feet, 2.5 inches
Wingspan:	32 feet, 4.5 inches
Wing Area:	176.53 square feet
Top Speed:	348 mph
Cruising speed:	300 mph
Max Ceiling:	34,450 feet
Range (max combat load):	412 miles
Armament:	2 machine guns
	2 cannons

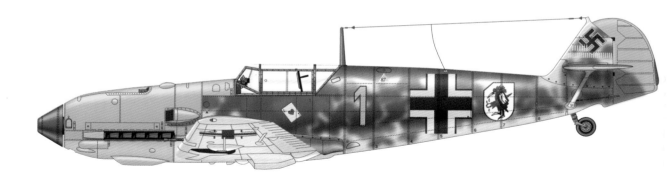

40

The Supermarine Spitfire

The Supermarine Spitfire remains one of the foremost and most popular aircraft designs ever. Its story started in 1931 when R.J. Mitchell responded to the publication of Air Ministry's specification F.7/30 which required the submission of designs for fighter aircraft capable of exceeding 251 mph. His first design, the Supermarine 224 flew in 1934. It was a great disappointment to Mitchell but his tenacity and unfailing spirit provoked him to develop instead an aircraft based on the Supermarine Schneider Trophy seaplane designs. Meanwhile, the Air Ministry accepted the Gloster Gladiator design and put this into production.

Mitchell's improved design won favour with the Air Ministry at the end of 1934 and in 1935 a contract was written for the development of that aircraft to meet a new specification, F10/35.

The Spitfire prototypes were all monoplanes with a closed cockpit and retractable undercarriage, hallmarks of designs required for the Air Force. These designs were to carry machine guns enclosed in the wings and to act as a short range high-performance interceptor. Mitchell continued to develop and improve his designs until his death in 1937 when Joseph Smith took over his mantle. His vision for slim wings of an elliptical design remained in place for many of the Spitfire marks which followed over the next ten years. The British public first saw the Spitfire at RAF Hendon's air display in June 1936. Production should have started immediately but Supermarine were already struggling to fulfil orders for the flying boats they were world renowned for.

At the start of the Battle of Britain there were 19 Spitfire squadrons. However this increased as production challenges were resolved and Spitfire availability increased. Despite this, it remained outnumbered by the Hawker Hurricane which had entered RAF service a year earlier. Throughout the summer of 1940 these two key aircraft gradually developed complementary roles as the Spitfire proved most capable of matching the performance of the Messerschmitt Bf 109 in performance and maneuverability. Both opponents combined small airframes with powerful V12 engines.

Early in its development, the Merlin engine's lack of a fuel injection system meant that both Spitfires and Hurricanes, unlike the Bf 109E, were unable to make steep nose-down dives. This meant a Luftwaffe fighter could simply "bunt" into a high-power dive to escape an attack, leaving the Spitfire behind. The effect of negative 'G' forces restricted the fuel supply to the Merlin engine. Spitfire pilots countered this by inverting the aircraft to follow their prey down, countering the negative G effect. It was believed that the carburettor increased the performance of the supercharger and thereby increased the power of the engine. This disadvantage existed until after the Battle of Britain, and finally in March 1941 an adaptation was made to partly cure the problem. Further improvements were introduced throughout the Merlin series until pressure carburettors were fitted in 1942.

The lower area of the Spitfire's cockpit showing the joy stick and rudder pedals

Due to a shortage of Browning machine guns, early Spitfires were fitted with only four guns, with the other four fitted later. Early tests showed that while the guns worked perfectly on the ground and at low altitudes, they tended to freeze at high altitude, especially the outer wing guns. Supermarine did not fix this problem until October 1938, when they added hot air ducts from the rear of the wing-mounted radiators to the guns (which

trapped hot air in the wing around the guns) and placed red fabric patches over the gun ports to protect the guns from cold, dirt and moisture until they were fired.

The first 310 Spitfires ordered were quoted as costing £4,500 each. When delivered, costs had risen to £5,333 each. By today's standards that was still a bargain!

To help build Spitfires in the numbers required, a new factory was opened at Castle Bromwich in late 1938 to supplement the efforts of Supermarine's main factory in Southampton. The new factory cost £4 million to build.

Because of the Spitfire's stressed-skin construction, local labour became a problem as the aircraft required precision engineering beyond the experience of normal labour forces. By May 1940, Castle Bromwich had not yet built its first Spitfire despite promises of producing 60 aircraft a week. Lord Beaverbrook, who was responsible for aircraft production handed the factory over to Lord Nuffield and transported skilled labourers from Southampton. The first Mark II Spitfires finally came off the production line at Birmingham in June 1940, just before the start of Britain's major hostilities. By June 1945 some 12,129 Spitfires had come off that production line: 4,489 Mark IIs, 5,665 Mark Vs, and 1,054 Mark XVIs.

Other Spitfire marks were dispersed to various factories around the country. Concerted efforts to bomb the main production lines at Woolston and Itchen near

Southampton were relatively unsuccessful until September when most of the major production jigs and machine tools had already been sent away. Dispersal went to airfields near to Eastleigh, Salisbury, Trowbridge and Reading.

All production Spitfires were flight tested before delivery. Jeffrey Quill oversaw that task with a team of twelve other test pilots during the Second World War. Quill was Vickers Supermarine's chief test pilot. When the last Spitfire rolled out in February 1948, some 20,351 airframes of all variants had been built, including twin-seat trainers. The Spitfire was the only British fighter aircraft to be in continuous production before, during and after the Second World War. The Spitfire was used by nearly all Britain's allies during the Second World War and remained in active service well into the 1950s, despite the development of jet propulsion.

A near to supersonic record

A Spitfire Mark XI flown by Sqn. Ldr. Martindale in April 1944 reached an airspeed of 606 mph. This was achieved as part of the tests being conducted at the time to try to break the sound barrier. The critical Mach number of the Spitfire's original elliptical wing was higher than the subsequently-used laminar-flow-section, straight-tapering-platform wing of the follow-on variants, proving that Mitchell's belief in this design being one of the ways to obtain high-speed flight, was correct.

Spitfire Marks which had been developed before the end of the Battle of Britain

Mark I
Engine: Total built: 1,577 (Jun 1936 to Aug 1940) Rolls-Royce Merlin II or III; Maximum power of 1,030 bhp; Maximum speed of 362 mph at 18,500 feet; Service ceiling of 34,500 feet; Rate of climb - 2,195 ft/min

Armament: 8 x .303 Browning Mark II machine guns (Mark 1A) or 4 x .303 Mark II machine guns and 2 x 20 mm Hispano cannon.

Mark II
Engine: Total built: 920 (1939-40) Rolls-Royce Merlin C liquid-cooled 27 litre V12; Maximum power of 900 bhp; Maximum speed of 349 mph at 16,800 feet; Service ceiling of 34,500 feet; Rate of climb - 1,770 ft/min

Armament: 8 x .303 Browning Mark II machine guns. The Mark II was very similar to the Mark 1 with a few select modifications.

Mark III
Total built: 2
The Mark III was a complete reworking of the Spitfire. It made its maiden flight on August 15th 1940. The N3297 had a top speed of 400 mph but it was unpopular with test pilots and all orders were cancelled before production.

43

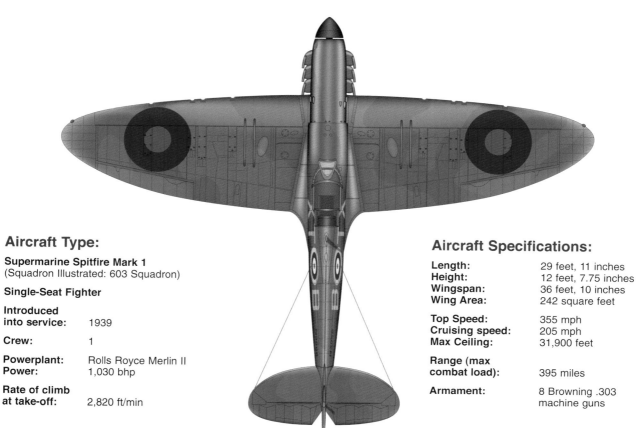

Aircraft Type:

Supermarine Spitfire Mark 1
(Squadron Illustrated: 603 Squadron)

Single-Seat Fighter

Introduced into service:	1939
Crew:	1
Powerplant:	Rolls Royce Merlin II
Power:	1,030 bhp
Rate of climb at take-off:	2,820 ft/min

Aircraft Specifications:

Length:	29 feet, 11 inches
Height:	12 feet, 7.75 inches
Wingspan:	36 feet, 10 inches
Wing Area:	242 square feet
Top Speed:	355 mph
Cruising speed:	205 mph
Max Ceiling:	31,900 feet
Range (max combat load):	395 miles
Armament:	8 Browning .303 machine guns

Junkers Ju 88

In August 1935, the German Air Ministry submitted its requirements for an unarmed, three-seat, high-speed bomber, with a payload of up to 2,200 lb.

Junkers presented their first design in June 1936, and were given clearance to build two prototypes. These had a range of 1,240 miles and were powered by two DB 600 engines.

Three more aircraft were developed, powered by Jumo 211 engines and having rear defensive armament in the rear of the cockpit. These first five prototypes had the qualities of a remarkably successful multi-role bomber that could obtain high speed (the fifth prototype attaining 320 mph with a payload of 2,200lb of bombs). Hermann Goering was said to be 'ecstatic'.

However, by the time the Luftwaffe had put in their modifications, the Ju 88's top speed had dropped to around 280 mph. Production was delayed drastically with developmental problems and the aircraft was not introduced into service until 1938, when initially only one aircraft per week was coming off the production line.

The first prototype to be tested as a dive-bomber was the Ju 88V4 followed by the V5 and V6. These models became the planned prototype for the A-1 series. Both the V5 and V6 were fitted with four-blade propellers, an additional bomb bay and a central control system. As a dive-bomber, the Ju 88 was capable of pinpoint deliveries of heavy loads but dive-bombing proved too stressful for the airframe, and in 1943, tactics were changed so that bombs were delivered from a shallower diving angle.

The Ju 88V7 was fitted with cable-cutting equipment to combat the potential threat of Barrage balloons and was successfully tested in this role. The V7 then had the Ju 88 A-1 nose installed with a defensive machine gun.

The maximum bomb load of the A-4 was 5,510 lb, but in practice, the standard bomb load was up to 4,410 lb. Junkers later used the A-4 design for the A-17 torpedo carrier. The standard fighter-bomber version became the Ju 88C-6, applying experience acquired with the A-4 bomber, equipped with the same Jumo 211J engines. The Ju 88C was originally intended as a fighter-bomber but became the first night-fighter variant with heavy defensive armour.

The Luftwaffe's order of battle for the French campaign reveals all but one of the Luftwaffe's Fliegerkorps (No 1) had Junkers Ju 88s in the front line. It proved to be especially successful as a dive-bomber in May 1940 when I and II/KG 54 flew 174 attacks against rail systems which helped to paralyse the French Army.

On 17 June 1940, Junkers Ju 88s from Kampfgeschwader 30 destroyed the RMS Lancastria liner, killing some 5,800 Allied personnel.

133 Ju 88s A-1s were used in Northern Europe as part of Blitzkrieg, but also suffered high losses, partly due to accidents. This was because the pilots found the Ju 88 difficult to fly in certain circumstances and many applied to transfer to Heinkel squadrons as a result. This resulted in the A-5 being quickly developed and sent to operational squadrons with many of the inherent problems being countered by a larger wingspan and a stronger air frame.

By August 1940, A-1 and A-5 variants were reaching operational units, just as the battle was intensifying. Although faster than the Dornier, its losses were higher than other bombers. Ju 88 losses over Britain in 1940 amounted to 313 aircraft between July-October 1940. Do 17 and He 111 losses for the same period amounted to 132 and 252 aircraft respectively. This was despite 'field kits' being issued to squadrons enabling them to replace the single rear machine gun by a twin-barrelled machine gun, and to install additional cockpit armour.

It was during the closing days of the Battle of Britain that the best variant of the Ju 88, the A-4 went into service. Although slower than the earlier A-1, other deficiencies in that model had been ironed out, making the A-4 a superb aircraft.

Ju 88D Cockpit: US Public Domain
www.nationalmuseum.af.mil

By the summer of 1941, most units equipped with the Dornier Do 17 were upgrading to the Ju 88. With a few exceptions, most of the German bomber units were now flying the He 111 and Ju 88. The Ju 88 was to prove a very capable and valuable asset to the Luftwaffe on the Eastern Front where, due to the lack of sufficient numbers of Ju 87 Stukas, the Ju 88 was also employed in a direct ground support role.

In April 1943, as Finland was still fighting its war against the USSR, the Finnish Air Force bought 24 Ju 88s from Germany and equipped No. 44 Squadron which had previously operated Bristol Blenheims. These were instead transferred to No. 42 Squadron.

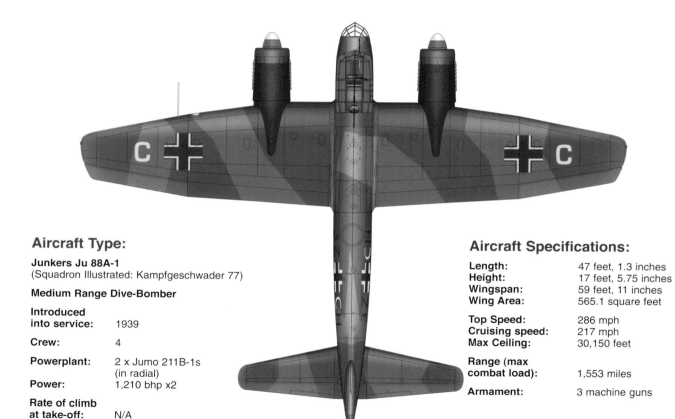

Aircraft Type:

Junkers Ju 88A-1
(Squadron Illustrated: Kampfgeschwader 77)

Medium Range Dive-Bomber

**Introduced
into service:** 1939

Crew: 4

Powerplant: 2 x Jumo 211B-1s
(in radial)

Power: 1,210 bhp x2

**Rate of climb
at take-off:** N/A

Aircraft Specifications:

Length: 47 feet, 1.3 inches
Height: 17 feet, 5.75 inches
Wingspan: 59 feet, 11 inches
Wing Area: 565.1 square feet

Top Speed: 286 mph
Cruising speed: 217 mph
Max Ceiling: 30,150 feet

**Range (max
combat load):** 1,553 miles

Armament: 3 machine guns

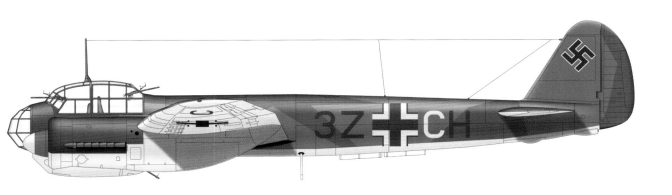

49

Dornier Do 17

Together with the Junkers Ju 86 and the Heinkel He 111, the Dornier Do 17 was designed in the early 1930s and produced as a civil aircraft before being adopted for military purposes.

The Do 17 was a fast, elegant two-engine aircraft built in response to a request by Deutsche Lufthansa for the construction of a fast postal plane capable of carrying six passengers.

It was as a combat plane that the Do 17 went down in aviation history, being one of the Luftwaffe's best known and most widely used aircraft on the European fronts. It was an aircraft that continued to evolve with numerous series, versions, and derivatives. It remained in production for the duration of the war and finally was found to have operated on practically all fronts.

The Dornier Do 17 project was begun in 1933. Three prototypes were completed in the course of the following year. However these aircraft were not considered suitable for commercial use for reasons that included the narrow fuselage which prevented passengers from being comfortably seated.

Although these prototypes were rejected, the potential of the aircraft remained significant and it was immediately transformed for military use. The fourth prototype appeared in the summer of 1935. It became the founder of a long series of bombers, whose initial production series (the E-1 and the F-1 reconnaissance versions) were also proven in combat in 1937 operating as part of the Condor Legion over Spain.

In addition to the advanced nature of its all-metal layout it was also a mid-wing monoplane with retractable landing gear. Its slim body gave it exceptional aerodynamics, enabling 'the flying pencil' to become well-known for its performance and speed.

After a series of minor variations the most widely produced variant was the Z, which went into service in 1939 and of which just over 500 were built up to the summer of 1940.

The Z series, as well as being the last model before the progression to the Dornier Do 217 (which was larger and more powerful), incorporated many modifications to the structure and configuration of the front part of the fuselage. This was to increase the efficiency of the rear ventral defensive position which was almost completely glazed to improve the bombardier's position.

The Do 17 Z-2 variant utilised more powerful engines (2 x 1,000 bhp BMW Bramo radial engines) which made it possible to increase the defensive armament to eight machine guns and the offensive armament to 2,200 lbs.

Other variants of the Dornier Do 17 included the Z-6 and Z-10 which were both designed as night bombers and fitted with heavy armament entirely in the nose cone. This consisted of three machine guns and a 20 mm cannon in the Do 17 Z-6 and four machine guns and two cannons in the Do 17 Z-10. Although the few aircraft built to this specification did not have an exten-

21 June 1940 - France - Dornier Do 17 Z-1 bombers in flight - *Bundesarchiv*

sive operational career, they made a valuable contribution to the development of techniques for this particular type of combat.

In 1939, just 370 Do 17s were in service in the Luftwaffe, of which two-thirds were of the Z series. These aircraft took part in all operations during the first two years of the war. Although sound aircraft they were not outstanding and specifically lacked the load capacity of the Heinkel He 111 and the speed of the Junkers Ju 88.

Dornier Do 17s were withdrawn from front-line service towards the end of 1942 when they were replaced by the more powerful and efficient Do 217s.

21 June 1940 - France - Dornier Do 17 bombers of KG 76 in flight; BGN Poland and KBK Lw.3 - *Bundesarchiv*

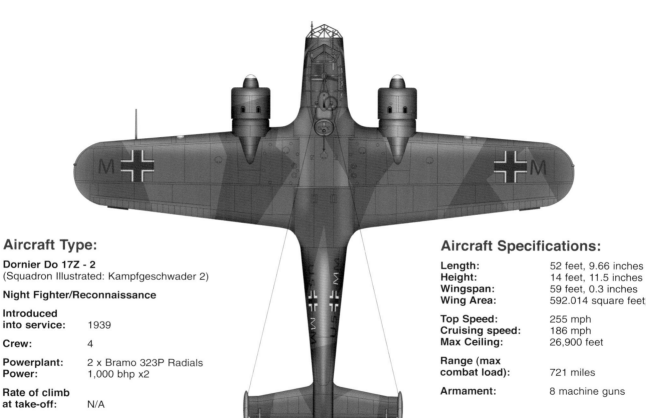

Aircraft Type:

Dornier Do 17Z - 2
(Squadron Illustrated: Kampfgeschwader 2)

Night Fighter/Reconnaissance

Introduced into service:	1939
Crew:	4
Powerplant:	2 x Bramo 323P Radials
Power:	1,000 bhp x2
Rate of climb at take-off:	N/A

Aircraft Specifications:

Length:	52 feet, 9.66 inches
Height:	14 feet, 11.5 inches
Wingspan:	59 feet, 0.3 inches
Wing Area:	592.014 square feet
Top Speed:	255 mph
Cruising speed:	186 mph
Max Ceiling:	26,900 feet
Range (max combat load):	721 miles
Armament:	8 machine guns

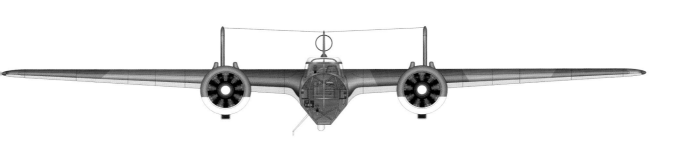

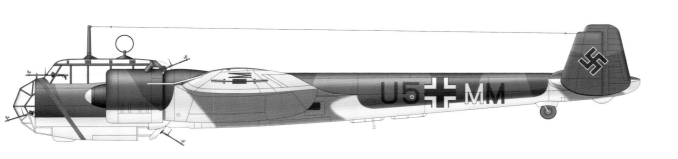

53

Heinkel He 111

Officially and originally designed as a civilian aircraft (in the same way as its contemporaries were: the Junkers Ju 86 and the Dornier Do 17), the Heinkel He 111 was perhaps the most successful representative of the deceptive rearmament policy carried out by Germany in the 1930s.

Like the other two aircraft, it was created to fulfil the dual role of being a fast commercial transport plane on the one hand and a medium-heavy bomber on the other. It was eventually to stand out for its true qualities as a combat plane more than as a transport or commercial aircraft. This occurred especially at a quantitative level, considering that production of this elegant two-engine aircraft continued from 1936 virtually up to the end of the war, totalling more than 7,300 in several variants.

He 111s were operational on all of Germany's war fronts in a variety of roles, proving the design's distinctive qualities even in the presence of more modern and battle-hardened aircraft.

The first prototype of the He 111 took to the air on February 24, 1935. The aircraft was clearly inspired by the single-engine Heinkel He 70, although it was much larger. It was followed by another two prototypes with a shorter wingspan. The fourth prototype became the

foundation for the civilian version, capable of carrying 10 passengers and a postal load. The aircraft was accepted in January 1936 when 10 aircraft were ordered, designated as the He 111C. These went into regular service with Lufthansa by the end of the year.

Following the disappointing performance of the third prototype (which was designed specifically for military use) in early 1936, a fifth experimental aircraft appeared. This led to the creation of the first bomber variant, the He 111B.

The Heinkel He 111B utilised two Daimler-Benz DB 600 engines. The aircraft went into service at the end of the year and in February 1937, 30 were assigned to the bomber division of the Condor Legion now operating in Spain.

On the assembly lines, military versions soon followed in quick succession. After only a few D series aircraft had been completed, a shortage of Daimler-Benz engines led to the development of the successive He 111E in which Junkers Jumo 211 engines were used.

The He 111G was characterized by substantial modifications to the wing structure, but it was in 1938, with the appearance of the prototypes of the P and H series, that the bomber assumed its definitive and most successful configuration. In these aircraft, the front part of the fuse-age was redesigned to be completely glazed and blended into the rest of the structure in order to allow the pilot and bomb aimer maximum visibility.

21 June 1940 - Heinkel He 111 bomber of KG 1 - *Bundesarchiv*

The He 111s used only the Jumo engine but increasingly powerful versions. The H series went into major production and entered service in May 1939. More than 800 were operational by September.

About 5,000 of this variant came off the production lines. After the H-2 and the H-3, one of the most widely used was the He 111 H-6, which appeared in 1941 specifically designed for naval warfare and used with great success as a torpedo launcher.

The 1943 H-10 and H-12 variants were noted by having increased bomb loads. Later, the Heinkel He 111 H-12

was modified to launch two radio-controlled Henschel Hs 293 missiles. The bomb load in the H-16 series reached 7,174 lb (3,250 kg).

The final He 111, the H-23 version, appeared in 1944. Its role was to transport and to release paratroopers.

The Heinkel He 111's career lasted well beyond World War II. In Spain, 263 H-16 variants were built on licence by CASA, and they remained in service throughout the 1960s demonstrating just how thorough the original conceptual designs had been in creating an aircraft able to adapt to the changing demands of time.

1939 - Construction of the Heinkel He 111 P-4 bomber (front), seen behind is the production of the Heinkel He 115 sea-plane. The He 111 P-4 was delivered 1939/40 and had the serial numbers 2906 - 3129. 2922 was therefore the 17th He 111 P-4 - *Bundesarchiv*

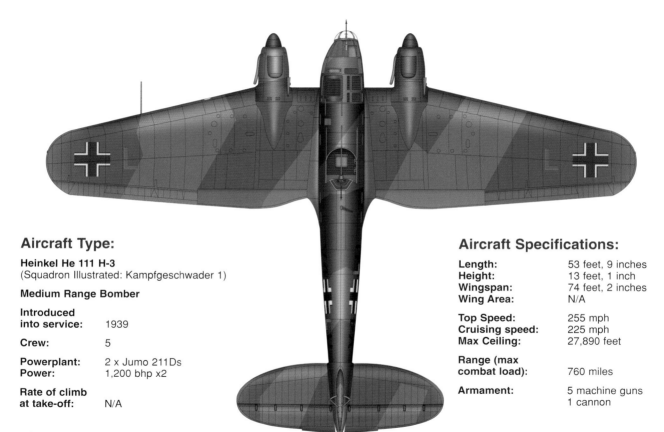

Aircraft Type:

Heinkel He 111 H-3
(Squadron Illustrated: Kampfgeschwader 1)

Medium Range Bomber

Introduced into service:	1939
Crew:	5
Powerplant:	2 x Jumo 211Ds
Power:	1,200 bhp x2
Rate of climb at take-off:	N/A

Aircraft Specifications:

Length:	53 feet, 9 inches
Height:	13 feet, 1 inch
Wingspan:	74 feet, 2 inches
Wing Area:	N/A
Top Speed:	255 mph
Cruising speed:	225 mph
Max Ceiling:	27,890 feet
Range (max combat load):	760 miles
Armament:	5 machine guns 1 cannon

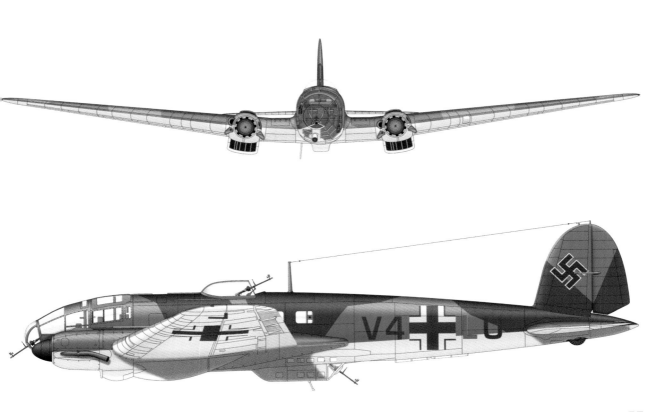

57

The Fairey Fulmar

The Fulmar was predominantly a British aircraft carrier-born fighter that served with the Fleet Air Arm (FAA). Although old in style it was a new aircraft, with the first production aircraft only becoming available from January 1940, when two squadrons of the two-seat fighter version became operational with 804 and 808 Squadrons.

The main design specification for the Fulmar had been that of a light bomber capable of being used as a dive-bomber. However, for this specification the as yet un-built Hawker Henley proved to be an aircraft, which offered better performance than the Fulmar, resulting in only 600 Fulmars being built when production was stopped in December 1942.

The Fulmar's design had been based on that of the Fairey P 4/34 which was in turn developed in 1936 as a replacement for the Fairey battle light bomber. Like its predecessors, the Fulmar lacked performance but was a reliable, sturdy aircraft with long range and an effective eight machine gun armament.

Although designed as a two-crew defence fighter, it was never realistically expected to encounter fighter opposition. High performance and maneuverability were not therefore considered as important as range and armament. The provision of a navigator/wireless operator was considered essential for long oceanic flights.

Fairey Battles remained in service while the Fulmar was coming off the same production lines. While looking much like the Battle, the Fulmar was more aerodynamically sound and featured a folding wing which was 16 inches shorter than the Battle bomber.

The first prototype had a 1,080 bhp Rolls Royce Merlin III engine. However for such a heavy aircraft, the Merlin III's performance was poor, enabling the aircraft to reach only 230 mph. Trials of the Merlin VIII increased this to 255 mph, which owing to the desperate need for modern fighters, was considered sufficient.

During testing, Fulmars were launched from catapults on merchant ships, a convoy defensive plan that was being evaluated at the time.

806 was the first Squadron to be equipped with the Fulmar, which was soon operating off the decks of HMS Illustrious. The Fulmar was not well matched for combat with land-based fighters though.

By 1942, the Fulmar was being replaced by single-seat aircraft adapted from land fighters including the Martlet and Seafire. It was used for service in night-time roles as a convoy escort. Approximately 100 Fulmars were converted into night fighters.

At one time, 20 Fleet Air Arm squadrons were equipped with the Fulmar which flew from eight fleet aircraft carriers and five escort carriers.

No. 273 Squadron of the RAF operated them for some months in 1942 from Ceylon, where they saw action against Japanese forces. Fulmars destroyed 112 enemy aircraft, which made it the leading fighter type in the Fleet Air Arm during the Second World War. The Fulmar ended its front line operational career on 8 February 1945, when a Fulmar Mark II night-fighter from No. 813 Squadron had a landing accident on the flight deck of HMS Campania.

Variants:

Mark I   First production variant powered by Rolls Royce Merlin VIII producing 1,035 bhp. 250 were built.

Mark II   Updated variant powered by a Merlin XXX producing 1,300 bhp. It had a new propeller and tropical equipment. Some were converted to night fighters. 350 were built.

Fleet Air Arm Squadrons equipped with Fulmars:

748	(Naval Fighter Pool)
759, 761	(RNAS Fighter School)
772, 775, 777	(Fleet Requirements Unit)
778	
784	(Night Fighter Training Unit)
787	(Fighter Development Unit)
795	(East African Fighter Pool)

Naval Air Squadrons:

800, 803, 804, 805, 806, 807, 808, 809
813   (Night Fighter)
884, 886, 887, 889

RAF Squadrons:

273 Squadron

The Aerodynamics of Flight

The basic aerodynamics of flight which applies to all aircraft are depicted here on the Fairey Fulmar.

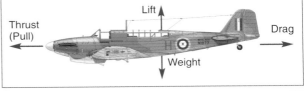

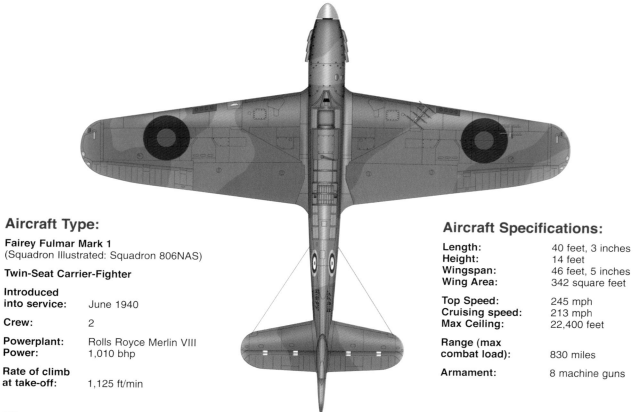

Aircraft Type:

Fairey Fulmar Mark 1
(Squadron Illustrated: Squadron 806NAS)

Twin-Seat Carrier-Fighter

Introduced into service:	June 1940
Crew:	2
Powerplant:	Rolls Royce Merlin VIII
Power:	1,010 bhp
Rate of climb at take-off:	1,125 ft/min

Aircraft Specifications:

Length:	40 feet, 3 inches
Height:	14 feet
Wingspan:	46 feet, 5 inches
Wing Area:	342 square feet
Top Speed:	245 mph
Cruising speed:	213 mph
Max Ceiling:	22,400 feet
Range (max combat load):	830 miles
Armament:	8 machine guns

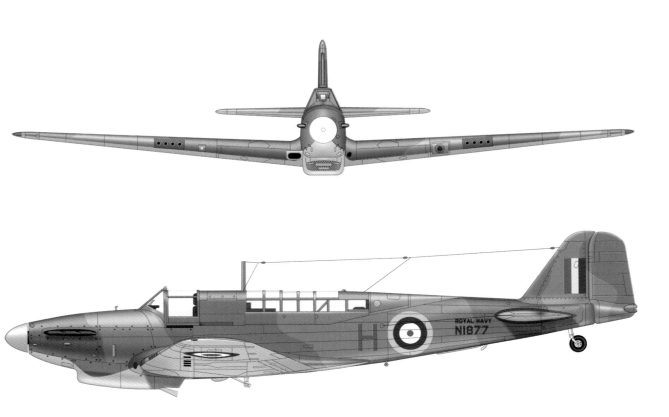

Gloster Gladiator

The Gladiator biplane was a single-seat aircraft initially developed as a private venture. However, it was found to conform to Air Ministry Specification F.7/30 of 1930 and soon became an RAF acquisition. The prototype flew in 1934 and production took place throughout 1935.

The aircraft was found to be highly maneuverable but its biplane design meant that it was soon superseded by monoplane fighter designs which emerged in the early 1930s.

During the Battle of Britain, the aircraft was still being used by 247 Squadron near Plymouth, partly due to its ability to land on grass strip airfields which were common in the south. Despite its aged design, it showed itself to perform reasonably well against the more advanced opposition it faced, although during the Battle of Britain did not account for any German losses.

Army Co-operation's 239 Squadron and the Fleet Air Arm's 804 Squadron were equipped with the Gladiator and Sea Gladiator respectively throughout the summer of 1940. It was also in use with many foreign Air Forces in the early 1940s though, including some Air Forces that fell under Axis control.

The Gladiator had been developed from Gloste Gauntlet. It met Aircraft Specification F.7/30 which demanded a top speed in excess of 250 mph from a fighter able to carry at least four machine guns.

Early engine experiments with Rolls Royce engines were unsuccessful so when the SS.37 prototype flew or 12 September 1934 it was powered by a 530 bhp Bristol Mercury engine. Subsequent aircraft had more powerful power plants and when the RAF commenced its evaluations it was using an 830 bhp Mercury IX engine.

The first version, the Mark I, was delivered to the RAF from July 1936 and became operational in January 1937. The Mark II followed with a slightly more powerful Mercury engine driving a fixed-pitch, three-bladed metal propeller instead of the two-bladed wooden one. A modified Mark II, the Sea Gladiator, was developed for the Royal Navy's Fleet Air Arm with an arrestor hook which engaged when landing on a carrier. Of the 98 aircraft built or converted to Sea Gladiators, 54 were still in service when Britain declared war on 3rd September 1939.

The Gladiator was the last British biplane fighter but also the first fighter with an enclosed cockpit. It had a top speed of around 257 mph. A total of 747 were built (483 for the RAF & 98 for the FAA). Of these, 216 were exported to 13 countries.

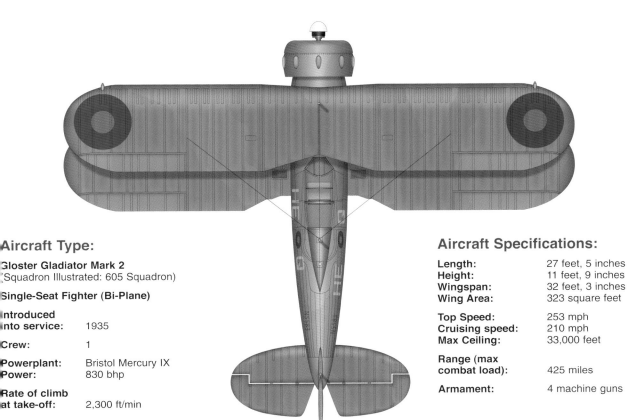

Aircraft Type:

Gloster Gladiator Mark 2
(Squadron Illustrated: 605 Squadron)

Single-Seat Fighter (Bi-Plane)

**Introduced
into service:**   1935

Crew: 1

Powerplant: Bristol Mercury IX
Power: 830 bhp

**Rate of climb
at take-off:**   2,300 ft/min

Aircraft Specifications:

Length: 27 feet, 5 inches
Height: 11 feet, 9 inches
Wingspan: 32 feet, 3 inches
Wing Area: 323 square feet

Top Speed: 253 mph
Cruising speed: 210 mph
Max Ceiling: 33,000 feet

**Range (max
combat load):**   425 miles

Armament: 4 machine guns

Most Gladiators were replaced in front-line RAF service by Hurricanes and Spitfires at the start of the Second World War. The Gloster Gladiator had performed reasonably well in limited Finnish service against Soviet fighters during the war against the Russians, but was outclassed by German fighters in other theatres or war. The carrier-based Sea Gladiators were more successful, since their slower speed made them more suitable for carrier operations and they were less likely to be facing more modern fighter opposition.

Other Operations
Belgian Gladiators suffered heavy losses during May 1940 with all 15 operational aircraft lost for managing to damage only two German aircraft. The Irish Air Corps were supplied with four Gladiators in March 1939. Two of these were scrambled in December 1940 to intercept a German Ju 88 flying over Dublin on a photographic reconnaissance mission, but they were unable to make contact. Ironically, the Luftwaffe used captured Latvian Gladiators as glider tugs during 1942-43.

After becoming obsolete, former front-line Gladiators carried out non-combat tasks such as meteorological work.

RAF Bomber Command

Fairey Battle Mark I

The Fairey Battle was designed in 1933 to replace the biplane light bombers that were still in RAF service at the time. It was clearly a transitional aircraft and proved to be unsuited to the new, more aggressive roles imposed by World War II. It was originally designed as a single-engine two-seat bomber capable of carrying a bomb load of 1,000 lb over a distance of 1,050 miles at speeds of up to 200 mph. The prototype was accepted by the RAF and then went into production, orders amounting to 655 aircraft. This number soon increased, so much so that the participation of other manufacturers in the production programme became necessary.

The Fairey Battle

The Battle was a large, low-wing, single-engine aircraft. Its three-man crew (pilot, gunner and radio operator) were accommodated in an expensive glazed cockpit. The bomb load was unusually contained inside the wings. The defensive armament consisted of a fixed machine gun in a half-wing and a flexible one in the rear.

The Battle was one of the first users of the Rolls-Royce Merlin engine, generating 1,030 bhp and driving a three-bladed, variable pitch metal propeller. The Battle was widely used during the early months of the war and especially in the Battle of France, during which it suffered heavy losses. Here, the aircraft's limitations became apparent as it was found to be unable to defend itself when attacked by enemy fighters.

As the Germans advanced in France, Battles were sent to help halt the advance. On 14 May 1940 during an attack on bridges and on German troops at Sedan, 40 of the 71 Battles taking part were shot down. The Battles were gradually withdrawn from front-line duty and from daylight operations.

Although modern in concept with an all-metal airframe and retractable landing gear, the Battle was already out-of-date by the time the war began, and its front line career lasted only for a year up to September 1940 at which point numbers produced totalled 2,185 aircraft.

Vickers Wellington

The Wellington was one of the best known and most widely used of the British bombers during the Second World War and until the appearance of the first heavy bombers such as the Short Stirling, the Handley Page Halifax, and the Avro Lancaster, it constituted the main strength of the RAF's Bomber Command.

The Wellington characterized military aviation in the 1930s and was a typical expression of the biplane formula. Although it shared the characteristics of many other models designed in various countries, the Vickers Wellington stood out as being a light aircraft of incredible strength. It was canvas covered, but despite this the Wellington proved capable of taking a remarkable amount of damage while still remaining airborne.

From 1937 to 1945, 11,461 aircraft were built in several versions acting as transport aircraft, light bombers and reconnaissance units, and with Coastal Command they were used in naval reconnaissance, submarine warfare and mine-laying.

The prototype made its first flight in June 1936, three and a half years after the project had got under way. By the end of the year, an order had been placed for 180 planes, and the first Wellington of the initial production series (the Mark I) appeared in December 1937. It was a mid-wing monoplane with retractable landing gear, powered by two 1,000 bhp Bristol Pegasus radial engines and capable of carrying 4,408 lb of bombs. Its defensive armament was remarkable too, with six 7.7 mm machine guns installed in two turrets in the nose, the tail and in two lateral positions.

Other variants followed. The Mark II series was powered by 1,145 bhp Rolls-Royce Merlin X liquid-cooled engines. Following the delivery of 200 Mark IVs, 3,803 Mark Xs were built with more powerful Bristol Hercules engines.

The Wellington's career with Bomber Command came to an end in October 1943. However, it was used in other theatres of war and served Coastal Command faithfully. The last Wellington, a Mark X, came off the assembly lines in October 1945.

Armstrong Whitworth Whitley

One of the oldest medium bombers in RAF service when the war broke out was the Armstrong Whitworth Whitley. Already outdated at the start of the war and therefore relegated to night missions, the Whitley had a long operating career in which 1,814 were built. They remained in front-line service with the units of Bomber Command until the spring of 1942, while those in Coastal Command were withdrawn in 1943. The Whitley

originated in 1934 when an initial order for 80 aircraft was placed before the prototypes had even flown.

It was a large, middle-wing twin-engine aircraft, with retractable landing gear and vertical twin rudders. Its most characteristic feature was its wings which were very thick with a large surface area installed at a sharp angle of incidence. This transformed the aircraft into adopting a "nose down" attitude during flight.

The first Mark I series aircraft were delivered at the beginning of 1937. The Mark IV, which made its maiden flight in April 1939 saw 40 built with different power plants (two Rolls-Royce Merlin V-12s).

The defensive armament was strengthened by a four machine gun tail turret. From this series the major production variant (the Mark V, of which 1,466 were built) then derived, featuring the installation of more powerful Merlin engines, as well as modification to the tail fins and fuselage. The final variant was the Mark VII, supplied to Coastal Command for the role of naval bomber and anti-submarine fighter.

Whitleys took part in all the major combat operations during the early years of the war and were the first British bombers to fly over Berlin on 1 October 1939, and the first to drop bombs on Italian territory in June 1940.

Other Aircraft

The vast majority of the aircraft that engaged in battle over the South of England during the summer of 1940 were those represented in the main body of this book. Numerous other aircraft types became embroiled in the events from time to time though, sometimes inadvertently.

Many aircraft were on the ground at RAF bases which were bombed in the early Luftwaffe actions, causing them to become among the first casualties. Others were reserved for special duties, such as coastal patrol, mine-laying and air-sea rescue.

The shortage of aircraft prior to 1939 meant that many aircraft which otherwise would have been replaced by more modern aircraft such as the Hurricane and Spitfire were still being flown operationally in 1939. These included the Westland Lysander (operating from RAF West Malling until Sept 1940) and the German equivalent, the Henschel Hs 126.

Both Air Forces were keen to recover as many pilots as possible from those lost over the English Channel. Despite being shot down and often badly wounded, experienced pilots were invaluable and were often able to be recovered by motor launches or floatplanes and subsequently returned to flying duties. For the RAF, the huge but incredibly inefficient Short Sunderland achieved this goal, while its German counterpart, the Heinkel He 59 conducted German mounted air-sea rescue operations alongside the Dornier Do 18 flying boat.

Variants of the more numerous aircraft also appeared in the battle, such as the Dornier 215 (which evolved from the Dornier 17) and Messerschmitt Bf 109G, which was a development from the highly successful Bf 109E and F variants. The Fairey Swordfish became fondly known as the Torpedo-Spotter Reconnaissance aircraft. It was simply a slow but multi-role aircraft. Then there was the Grumman Martlet Mark 1, a twin-seat fighter which crept into service with the RAF just before the Battle of Britain ended as a powerful and sturdy replacement for the Fairey Fulmar.

Even a training aircraft, an Avro Tutor saw action – Sergeant B. Hancock of No. 6 SFTS (training Squadron) heroically flew his Avro trainer into the path of an incoming Heinkel 111 bomber which was lining up to bomb his airfield.

Two Italian aircraft, the Fiat CR 52 Fighter and BR20 bomber saw limited action too once Italy had formally joined Germany to create the basis of the Axis forces. The Fiats were employed by the Luftwaffe Group operating out of Norway to attack the North of Britain.

	Messerschmitt Bf 109 F-1 ✚ Single-Seat Escort Fighter	Messerschmitt Bf 110 C-4B ✚ Long Range Fighter Bomber	Fiat CR42 FRECCIA (Arrow) ✚ Single-Seat Fighter (Bi-Plane)	Junkers Ju 87 R-2 Stuka ✚ Precision Dive Bomber
Introduced into service:	1940	October 1940	UK Operational October 1940	1938
Crew:	1	2-3	1	2
Powerplant: Power:	Daimler Benz DB 601E 1,350 bhp	2 x Daimler Benz DB 601Ns 1,100 bhp x 2	Fiat A.74R1C-38 Radial 840 bhp	Junkers Jumo211 J 1,200 bhp
Rate of climb at take-off:	N/A	2,165 ft/min	2,363 ft/min	1,640 ft/min
Length: Height: Wingspan: Wing Area:	29 feet, 7.2 inches 8 feet, 2.5 inches 32 feet, 6.5 inches 176.53 square feet	39 feet, 8.5 inches 13 feet, 6.5 inches 53 feet, 4.75 inches 413.33 square feet	27 feet, 3 inches 11 feet, 9 inches 31 feet, 10 inches N/A	36 feet, 5 inches 13 feet, 2 inches 45 feet, 3.5 inches 343.37 square feet
Top Speed: Cruising speed: Max Ceiling:	354 mph N/A 38,000 feet	336 mph 217 mph 32,000 feet	272 mph 232 mph 33,500 feet	255 mph Dive speed 404 mph 26,250 feet
Range (max combat load):	525 miles with drop tanks	680 miles	480 miles	779 miles with drop tanks
Armament:	2 machine guns 1 cannon	4 machine guns 2 cannons	2 machine guns	3 machine guns, 1 moveable, 2 fixed
Max Bomb Load:	N/A	2 x 550 lb bombs	N/A	2,205 lb

	Dornier Do 18D-1 Minelaying/ Reconnaissance	Fiat BR20 (M) CICIGNA (Stork) Twin-Engined Bomber	Dornier Do 17Z -2 Medium Range Bomber	Heinkel He 59 Rescue Float Plane/Torpedo Bomber
Introduced into service:	1940	UK Operational Oct 1940	1939	N/A
Crew:	4	5	4	3
Powerplant: **Power:**	2 x Junkers 205 C 605 bhp x 2	2 x Fiat A.80 R.C. 41 Radials 1,030 bhp x 2	2 x Bramo 323P Radial 1,000 bhp x 2	2 x BMW VIs 660 bhp x 2
Rate of climb at take-off:	N/A	N/A	N/A	656 ft/min
Length: **Height:** **Wingspan:** **Wing Area:**	63 feet, 1 inch 17 feet, 5.75 inches 77 feet, 9 inches 1,055 square feet	52 feet, 10 inches 14 feet, 1 inch 70 feet, 8 inches N/A	52 feet, 9.66 inches 14 feet, 11.5 inches 59 feet, 0.3 inches 592.014 square feet	57 feet, 0.75 inches 23 feet, 3.5 inches 77 feet, 9 inches 1,648.5 square feet
Top Speed: **Cruising speed:** **Max Ceiling:**	155 mph (at sea level) N/A 14,270 feet	286 mph 220 mph 29,500 feet	255 mph 186 mph 33,500 feet	137 mph 106 mph 16,404 feet
Range (max combat load):	2,175 miles	1,860 miles	721 miles	1,175 miles
Armament:	2 machine guns	3 machine guns	8 machine guns	None
Max Bomb Load:	220 lb	3,527 lb	N/A	N/A

	Dornier Do 17P	Heinkel He 111 P-4	Dornier Do 215 B-1	Fairey Battle
	Night Fighter/ Reconnaissance	Medium Range Bomber	Medium Range Bomber	Light Bomber
Introduced into service:	1937	1939	1937	1937
Crew:	4-5	5	4	3
Powerplant: Power:	2 x BMW 132 Ns 840 bhp	2 x Daimler Benz DB 601s 1,100 bhp x 2	2 x Daimler Benz DB 601BAs 1,175 bhp x 2	Rolls Royce Merlin Mark 1 1,030 bhp
Rate of climb at take-off:	N/A	937 ft/min	N/A	N/A
Length: Height: Wingspan: Wing Area:	53 feet, 3.75 inches 14 feet, 2 inches 59 feet, 0.75 inches 592 square feet	57 feet, 5 inches 13 feet, 1.5 inches 74 feet, 2 inches 942.917 square feet	51 feet, 9.67 inches 14 feet, 11.5 inches 59 feet, 0.67 inches 592 square feet	52 feet, 1 inch 15 feet, 6 inches 54 feet 422 square feet
Top Speed: Cruising speed: Max Ceiling:	236 mph N/A 18,050 feet	200 mph 193 mph 25,000 feet	314 mph N/A 29,500 feet	241 mph N/A 23,500 feet
Range (max combat load):	745 miles	760 miles	1,522 miles	1,050 miles
Armament:	7 machine guns	3 machine guns 2 cannons in nose	6 machine guns	2 machine guns
Max Bomb Load:	N/A	1,322 lb	2,205 lb	500 lb

	Avro Anson ◉ Multi-Role Fighter/ Light Bomber	Hawker Hurricane Mark II ◉ Single-Seat Fighter	Grumman Martlet Mark 1 ◉ Carrier-Fighter	Supermarine Spitfire Mark II ◉ Single-Seat Fighter
Introduced into service:	1936	August 1940	October 1940	August 1940
Crew:	3	1	1	1
Powerplant:	2 x Armstrong Siddeley Cheetah IX	Rolls Royce Merlin XX	Wright Cyclone G-205 A	Rolls Royce Merlin XII
Power:	350 bhp x 2	1,185 bhp	1,000 bhp	1,175 bhp
Rate of climb at take-off:	750 ft/min	2,380 ft/min	2,325 ft/min	2,925 ft/min
Length: Height: Wingspan: Wing Area:	42 feet, 3 inches 13 feet, 1 inch 56 feet, 6 inches 463 square feet	31 feet, 5 inches 12 feet, 11.5 inches 40 feet 258 square feet	28 feet, 9 inches 9 feet, 3 inches 38 feet 260 square feet	29 feet, 11 inches 12 feet, 7.75 inches 36 feet, 10 inches 242 square feet
Top Speed: Cruising speed: Max Ceiling:	188 mph N/A 19,000 feet	342 mph 232 mph 35,000 feet	325 mph 285 mph 28,400 feet	370 mph 215 mph 37,600 feet
Range (max combat load):	790 miles	600 miles	1,150 miles	500 miles
Armament:	N/A	8 machine guns	4 machine guns	8 machine guns
Max Bomb Load:	N/A	N/A	N/A	N/A

	Sea Gladiator — Single-Seat Fighter (Bi-Plane)	Bristol Blenheim 1 — Twin-Engined Fighter/Bomber	Fairey Swordfish — Torpedo Bomber	Westland Lysander Mark III — Multi-Role Co-Operation Plane
Introduced into service:	1939	1937	1936	1936
Crew:	1	3	3	1
Powerplant: Power:	Bristol Mercury VIIIA 840 bhp	2 x Bristol Mercury VIIIs 840 bhp x 2	Bristol Pegasus III M 690 bhp	Bristol Mercury XV A 905 bhp
Rate of climb at take-off:	2,300 ft/min	1,480 ft/min	N/A	1,250 ft/min
Length: Height: Wingspan: Wing Area:	27 feet, 5 inches 11 feet, 9 inches 32 feet, 3 inches 323 square feet	39 feet, 9 inches 9 feet, 10 inches 56 feet, 4 inches 469 square feet	35 feet, 8 inches 12 feet, 4 inches 45 feet, 6 inches 607 square feet	30 feet, 6 inches 14 feet, 6 inches 50 feet 260 square feet
Top Speed: Cruising speed: Max Ceiling:	245 mph 212 mph 32,000 feet	263 mph 215 mph 27,280 feet	139 mph N/A 19,250 feet	212 mph N/A 21,500 feet
Range (max combat load):	425 miles	1,480 miles	546 miles	600 miles
Armament:	4 machine guns	2 machine guns	2 machine guns	4 machine guns
Max Bomb Load:	N/A	1,000 lb	1,670 lb	N/A

	Short Sunderland Mark 1 Multi-Role Flying Boat	Vickers Wellington Mark III Medium Bomber
Introduced into service:	1935	1939
Crew:	8-11	6
Powerplant:	4 x Pratt & Whitney Wasps	2 x Hercules XI radials
Power:	1,200 bhp x 4	1,389 bhp x 2
Rate of climb at take-off:	720 ft/min	1,120 ft/min
Length:	85 feet, 4 inches	60 feet, 11 inches
Height:	32 feet, 10.5 inch	17 feet, 5 inches
Wingspan:	112 feet, 9.5 inches	86 feet, 4 inches
Wing Area:	1,487 square feet	840 square feet
Top Speed:	213 mph	254 mph
Cruising speed:	178 mph	N/A
Max Ceiling:	16,000 feet	19,050 feet
Range (max combat load):	1,780 miles	1,539 miles
Armament:	18 machine guns	8 machine guns
Max Bomb Load:	N/A Variants evolved	4,500 lb

Combat Turning Circles

Comparing the turning circle and G force of the Battle of Britain's top three fighters (all comparisons based on half fuel load).

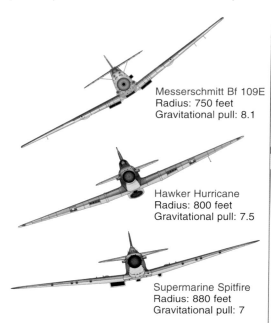

Messerschmitt Bf 109E
Radius: 750 feet
Gravitational pull: 8.1

Hawker Hurricane
Radius: 800 feet
Gravitational pull: 7.5

Supermarine Spitfire
Radius: 880 feet
Gravitational pull: 7

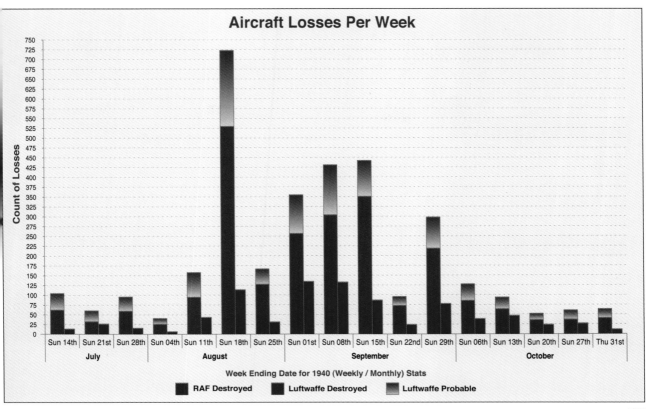

Aircraft Losses Per Week

Count of Losses

July	August	September	October
Sun 14th, Sun 21st, Sun 28th	Sun 04th, Sun 11th, Sun 18th, Sun 25th	Sun 01st, Sun 08th, Sun 15th, Sun 22nd, Sun 29th	Sun 06th, Sun 13th, Sun 20th, Sun 27th, Thu 31st

Week Ending Date for 1940 (Weekly / Monthly) Stats

■ RAF Destroyed   ■ Luftwaffe Destroyed   ■ Luftwaffe Probable

75

Aircraft Comparative Sizes

The aircraft which fought in the Battle of Britain varied significantly in size and in the levels of defensive armament they carried. They also varied in the amount of damage they could sustain. These pages compare the aircraft by size.

Gloster Gladiator Mark 2: 27 feet, 5 inches

Supermarine Spitfire Mark 1: 29 feet, 11 inches

Hawker Hurricane Mark 1: 31 feet, 5 inches

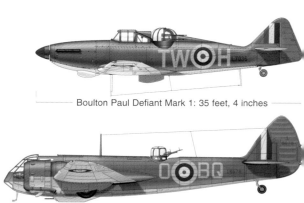
Boulton Paul Defiant Mark 1: 35 feet, 4 inches

Bristol Blenheim Mark 1: 39 feet, 9 inches

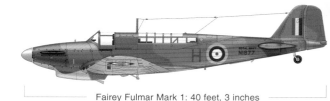
Fairey Fulmar Mark 1: 40 feet, 3 inches

Messerschmitt Bf 109E: 28 feet, 4.25 inches

Junkers Ju 88A-1: 47 feet, 1.3 inches

Junkers Ju 87B-1 Stuka: 36 feet, 1 inch

Dornier Do 17P: 53 feet, 3.75 inches

Messerschmitt Bf 110C-1: 39 feet, 8.5 inches

Heinkel He 111 H-3: 53 feet, 9 inches

77

Books
Available individually or as a commemorative pack:
Flying For Freedom – A Pilot's Story
The Battle of Britain –
    A Definitive Chronology of Events
The Battle of Britain – A Timeline of Events
Aircraft of the Battle of Britain
Battlefield Britain
Opposing Genius
Pilots of the Battle of Britain
Radar and the Secret Wireless War
Spitfire Pilot

Available individually or as a twin-set:
Allied Fighter Aces of World War 2
American Pilots of the Battle of Britain

Limited Edition Artwork
Spitfires 'Line-A-Stern'

'In – Readiness' (Spitfire on Airstrip)
'Into the Battlezone'
The Legendary 109
Hurricane!
Their Finest Hour Artwork 3D
Their Finest Hour 'Aircraft of the Battle of Britain'
Postcards

DVDs
Battlefield Britain	2 x 90 minutes
Aircraft of the Battle of Britain	3 x 60 minutes
Opposing Genius	1 x 60 minutes
Pilots of the Battle of Britain	1 x 75 minutes
The Civilian War	1 x 60 minutes
Britain Stands Alone	3 x 60 minutes
Spitfire!	1 x 60 minutes

Limited Edition 'Spitfire' Smart Cars
Yes, 10 'Their Finest Hour' officially branded smart cars.
Personalised to incorporate the initials of purchaser.
(Finance available, subject to status)

Music CDs
The 1940s Collection: 3 CDs brought together as a
musical tribute to the era in one pack:
Dame Vera Lynn's 'White Cliffs of Dover'
Dorothy Lamour's 'Thanks for the Memory'
Glenn Miller's 'Moonlight Serenade'

A4 and A5 Aircraft Illustrations

(Available individually or as a set of 12)
Supermarine Spitfire Mark 1, Hawker Hurricane Mark 1, Boulton Paul Defiant, Gloster Gladiator, Fairey Fulmar, Bristol Blenheim, Messerschmitt Bf 109E, Messerschmitt Bf 110C, Heinkel He 111 Bomber, Junkers Ju 87 'Stuka' Dive Bomber, Junkers Ju 88 Bomber, Dornier Do 17 Bomber

Die Cast Models (1/72 Scale)

Supermarine Spitfire, Hawker Hurricane, Junkers Ju 87 'Stuka' Dive Bomber, Messerschmitt Bf 109E

Plastic Models

Messerschmitt Bf 109E	1/24, 1/48, 1/72 scale
Junkers Ju 87-B 'Stuka'	1/24, 1/48, 1/72 scale
Supermarine Spitfire Mark 1	1/24, 1/48, 1/72 scale
Hawker Hurricane	1/24, 1/72 scale

Other models (1/72 Scale)

Heinkel He 111 Bomber, Junkers Ju 88 Bomber, Messerschmitt Bf 110C, Gloster Gladiator, Boulton Paul Defiant, Fairey Fulmar (FAA), Bristol Blenheim, Dornier Do 17

Sets in 1/72 Scale

Battle of Britain Airfield Set, Luftwaffe Airfield Set, RAF Airfield Set

'Dogfight Double' - Junkers Ju 88 and Hawker Hurricane

Battle of Britain 70th Anniversary Set - Heinkel He 111 Bomber, Hawker Hurricane, Supermarine Spitfire and Messerschmitt Bf 109E

Battle of Britain Commemorative Set - Supermarine Spitfire, Hawker Hurricane, Junkers Ju 87 'Stuka' Dive Bomber and Heinkel He 111 Bomber

Memorabilia and Coasters

1940s coins, stamps and other items, plus Battle of Britain coasters and original pieces of memorabilia

**All 'TFH' products available
from the TFH official Website.
Subject to Availability.**

**www.theirfinesthour.co.uk or email:
products@theirfinesthour.co.uk**